How the West Was One

A non-fairytale love story infused with poetry, affirmations, narrations, and acts of resilience.

I0539466

WALTER & CHARMAINE JENNINGS
Relationship Specialists

RAIN
PUBLISHING

TAMPA, FL

How the West Was One by Walter and Charmaine Jennings
Rain Publishing
www.rainpublishing.com

Visit the Author's Website at chosenlifespecialists.com
Cover Design by Charmaine Jennings

How the West was One/Walter and Charmaine Jennings
ISBN: 979-8-218-49093-5

To Charmione & Simone:

This book is intended to be a documentation of our love story. However, the two of you are the fruit of our love. The Lord has blessed us with the opportunity to serve so many people throughout our lives, but our greatest honor has been the responsibility of being your parents.

We were always under the impression that it was our job to instruct and train you. However, we quickly realized that it was YOU who were sent to teach us…and we have learned so many lessons: childproofing is a myth, stay calm during hypotheticals and "what if" scenarios, pick the right hair stylists, always switch up hiding places for snacks, know your children's friends, embrace the power of giving money versus giving presents, and grandparents are enablers.

If there is anything that we pray you take from our role in your lives, it is to always hold firm to your faith. Trust the Lord to order your steps and believe that He will guide and direct you in the way you need to go. We may have fallen short (often!) but know that God is faithful and will never fail you!

When the Lord gives you children, He hands you a mirror. Thank you for being a beautiful reflection of our strengths, challenges, and God's eternal love for us.

Love,
Mom & Dad

"If LOVE is defined as giving someone the power to destroy you and trusting that they will not do it... We should also define LOVE as giving someone the power to build you up and trust that they will become a loyal partner in the long journey ahead." ~Walter & Charmaine Jennings

LEMONADE & SWEET TEA CONTENTS

PREFACE

INTRODUCTION: Uhhh...Who Are They Again?!

    1.   About Walter

    2.   About Charmaine

    3.   His 6 Word Story

    4.   Her 6 Word Story

CHAPTER 1: THE DEBUTANTE DOUBLE TAKE   1

    1.   How We Met? His Side   3

    2.   How We Met? Her Side   5

    3.   The Soundtrack Of My Life by Wally-B   7

    4.   Maine Street by C-Maine   15

CHAPTER 2: COLLEGE, CAMO, & COLD-BLOODED MURDER   19

    1.   Red Flags: Love Impossible by C-Maine   29

    2.   Quiz: Detecting Red Flags   31

    3.   I Used to Love Him Poem by C-Maine   33

    4.   Stuck In My Mind by Wally-B   37

    5.   Never Say Never: Bloody Murder by C-Maine   41

CHAPTER 3: THE WEDDING OF A LIFETIME...OR NOT   47

    1.   Misplaced Emotion by Wally-B   53

    2.   I Don't Need A Diamond. I Am One! by C-Maine   57

    3.   PreNuptial Disagreement by Wally-B   61

CHAPTER 4: MARRIAGE FOR DUMMIES: *Young, Dumb & In Love*   65

    1.   Incinerating Perry Ellis Slacks by Wally-B   71

    2.   Rings, Dresses & Fondant Dreams by C-Maine   75

    3.   Paint By Numbers by Wally-B   79

CHAPTER 5: THE DRAMA OF TRAUMA: *Liquor & Lick Her Secrets*   85

    1.   Trauma by C-Maine   87

    2.   You Are Victorious   89

    3.   Slave Style by Wally-B   93

    4.   Break Down by C-Maine   95

    5.   Self-Analysis by Wally-B   103

    6.   Letters of the Lost by C-Maine   107

CHAPTER 6: CHILDREN AIN'T KIDS!   113

    1.   The Declaration of Dependents by Wally-B   117

    2.   Beautiful Surprise by C-Maine   121

    3.   God Gave Me Girls by Wally-B   127

    4.   Daughter Diaries by C-Maine   131

CHAPTER 7: RELATION...SLIPS: *Ignorance is Bliss or Causes Blisters*   135

    1.   Love's Inspiration by Wally-B   139

    2.   Just Want to Love You by C-Maine   145

    3.   Cheaters Never Win 2.0 by C-Maine   149

CHAPTER 8: TAP DANCING ON MY HAIKU NERVES: *Are We Gon Make It?* 153

    1.   Quiz: A Pet Peeve, Petty or Passive   155

    2.   His Haiku Nerves   157

    3.   Her Haiku Nerves   159

CHAPTER 9: ODE TO RELATIONSHIPS LETTER   161

    Dear Men...   163

    Dear Women...   165

CHAPTER 10: IF I KNEW THEN...WHAT I KNOW NOW   167

    Words of Wisdom

ABOUT THE AUTHORS & APPRECIATION

PREFACE

Well, Well, Well! You made it! Welcome! The good news is that you accepted the challenge to read this unique book. The less-than-positive news is, if you are expecting a sappy fairytale narrative with a cute happily-ever-after ending, then pick another book to read! Take a breath! You made the right decision.

In fact, if you're reading this, then you've probably already discovered the painful truth about love and relationships: Reality very rarely aligns with "Fantasy." All those Disney movies, romance novels, and social media posts filled you with expectations based on sensationalism and short-sighted perspectives.

The Truth? Love is the most beautiful experience unimaginable to the naked eye. It is euphoria wrapped in liberation that can be felt, yet too complex to fully explain. It is also the messiest, ugliest depiction of our most authentic selves when forgiveness is absent. It is insomnia caused by regret. Love leaves dark circles or bags underneath both eyes when countless tears pay homage to grief. Ironically, this intense dynamic is what makes us simultaneously pursue and despise love. If we attempt to ignore or abandon it, the urge grows stronger within us.

This book chronicles the journey of two individuals committed to embracing this tumultuous yet rewarding path. Their goal is to use their experience as a testimony to inspire you to love, embrace the truth, accept the work, and embody valor. Believe in the desired outcome for you and your relationship.

If you can handle the truth... get ready to quench the heat with south-ern iced tea, freshly squeezed lemonade, and a tall glass of westside reality. This story has never been fully disclosed for public consump-tion. It is an exclusive and has been generously placed into your hands. Drink up!

Walter and Charmaine Jennings
West Tampa and West Palm Beach, Florida

⌘

INTRODUCTION
UHHH...Who Are They Again?!

Walter	Charmaine
Wally-B	C-Maine
West Tampa, Florida	West Palm Beach, Florida
Sweet Tea	Lemonade
Navy Blue	Purple
Seafood	Seafood
Strawberry Fruit Rollups	Werther's Butterscotch
"The fleas come with the dog."	"There is no crown without a cross."
Dr. Martin Luther King	
	Rita Pierson
The Alchemist	
	The Book of James
Someone Suffering from My Mistake	
	A Broken Family
Romantic Walk On The Beach At Night	
	Magical Kiss Under The Moonlight
Triangle	
	Squiggly

SIX WORD (LIFE) STORIES

Raised In
Church.
Left.
Found God.

Jamaican
Roots.
Florida Palms.
Village Raised.

⌘

CHAPTER ONE
The Debutante
Double Take

THERE ARE ALWAYS THREE SIDES TO A "HOW WE MET" STORY

HIS SIDE

I was really looking forward to going down to West Palm Beach for a couple of different reasons:

#1 - I was a junior in college at Florida A&M University and we were on a winter break. West Palm Beach was one of my favorite cities to spend time in.

#2 - I was going to escort my godsister to a debutante ball. Honestly, I actually like "cleaning up" and attending formal events. There's something about the attire and atmosphere of it all. I think it's really cool.

#3 - I had just gotten out of a two-year relationship. I was looking forward to having fun, enjoying myself, and putting that relationship behind me. I had one of my good friends travel with me. We arrived in the city late, so we had to head straight over to the hotel for rehearsal. There's always this intrigue when you're around people (girls) that you don't know. You're watching but you're also watching to see who's watching you. Now, I have to be honest, I had my eye set on another young lady who was participating in the debutante ball. I thought she was really cute; however, after we had our initial practice, I saw her in the mall getting her nails done and she seemed really pretentious. I was immediately turned off. Call it short-sighted or discerning, but sometimes you just know. Anyway, we went through with the debutante ball, and it was a great experience. Afterward, some parents of one of the students who were involved hosted a late-night breakfast for all of us to hang out. We got a chance to eat fish, play cards, and just kick it. My godsister and I were playing cards and this young lady walked through the door. She was absolutely beautiful! But it wasn't just about how she "looked;" it was how she carried herself. Basically, it was the complete opposite experience from the girl getting her nails done. I asked my godsister who she was, and it turned out that the young lady had participated in the ball as well! In fact, she was going to be spending the night with us in the suite that my godparents had gotten for all of us. Honestly, I was more intrigued than excited. I was curious to see how she moved in general around a group of people to help determine if I would even want to ask her out for a date. I was hopeful.

Well, the breakfast came to an end and a group of about 6 of us went back to the suite. Everyone was still wired and wide awake from the day, so we decided to play a game of truth or dare. I'm not sure why or how, but somehow during the first rotation…Charmaine took a dare from me: She proceeded to go out on the balcony and at the top of her lungs…sing her school alma mater…at like 2:00 am. First off, who actually knows the words to their alma mater? Second, she sang it with an opera voice. Needless to say, I was smitten! When the second rotation came around, I decided to ask her out on a date. Why did I do this during the game?

A) I was nervous. B) She didn't know me, so there wasn't a guarantee that I would have the time or space to ask her in private. C) I was nervous. D) I figured I stood a better chance of getting a "yes" if I asked her in front of other people. E) I was nervous. It was slow and awkward, but she eventually said "yes." Thus began the journey of our relationship.

HER SIDE

My mother made me do it! Okay, not really but she was very excited for me to have the experience. I was invited to be a debutante and answered the call. Although it was a new endeavor, I embraced the adventure. It was definitely outside of my comfort zone. It required me to wear a huge white ballroom gown, to learn how to ballroom dance and to ask a boy to be my date. This did not represent me in my most organic self, but this experience would be an opportunity for my mother and I to connect in a new way.

There was a lot of preparation leading up to the event, but the night of the ball was magical. Everything was smooth and falling into place. During the event, I observed the date of a fellow friend, named Fredara Hadley. She was being escorted by her godbrother from Tampa, Florida. I noticed that he was the only guy in the ball without a tuxedo. In that moment, I made a mini judgment that was never spoken out loud, but definitely a thought. My judgment was that he seems like a guy who loves the spotlight. I would later learn that he was a college student with a limited budget.

Later that night after the debutante ball, we were invited to the home of a Bridge Club member for an after-party. The event sponsor served us southern-style fish and grits and allowed us to hang out and play cards (i.e. spades). My band sister and I arrived about 45 minutes late. We both were too shy to knock on the door after hearing the laughter and music vibrating from the windows. Once we mustered up the nerve to knock, the "ROTC uniform-wearing college" guy invited us to sit at the card table. We immediately started playing cards and he seemed friendly. Afterwards, my band sister and I drove around town to find other social spots with the other ball attendees.

While parked in front of a nightclub that we were too young to get into, I saw him smoking a cigar and drinking. My next judgment was, he seems nice but possibly a bad boy type, which isn't my preferred cup of lemonade.

Later that night, I realized that we were all going to be staying in the same hotel room because I was invited to spend the night with Fredara. During a crazy game of truth or dare, the "ROTC uniform-wearing, bad boy guy, spotlight lover," dared me to sing my high school's alma mater. I gladly obliged, went out on the balcony of the hotel room, and belted out the verses in an opera voice. I enjoyed making everyone laugh, but the second round came, and he said, truth or dare. This time I selected the truth. He chose that moment to ask me out on a date. Wow! I had never been asked out in a room full of people.

This was awkward because there was another girl in the room who liked him. I told him I wasn't sure because it depended on what they had going on. He seemed clueless about her. The "ROTC uniform-wearing, bad boy, spotlight lover, oblivious about girl crushes" guy assured me that there wasn't anything going on. Fredara convinced me that he was a genuinely nice guy. He assured me that he wanted to go out on a date with me and that there was no conflict, so I said, "yes." My response led to a wonderful first date that ended with a tender kiss on a moonlit beach in my hometown.

THE SOUNDTRACK OF MY LIFE

December 30th
1976.
The year I came to exist
also saw "Rubberband Man" by the Spinners become a national hit
…thus predicts the story of my life,
able to bounce back after my brother saw me for the first time and
told my parents to take me back to the hospital because he thought
I was white,
and even though I didn't know it then,
that comment started the journey of me always trying to figure out
where I fit in.
…quiet, shy, and reserved,
a demeanor that left my parents perturbed
because the two siblings above me had no problems expressing
how they feel…
okay,
I'm being nice,
they were hell-on-wheels,
and since I seemed to be an anomaly
the speculation was that I was probably…you know… "special,"
in a "short bus with tinted windows" kinda way,
my mother had me at 34 so maybe they waited too late,
but after high marks on my IQ test
any thoughts about mental instability were put to rest,
regularly dressed
with a Jimmie Giles/Buccaneers T-shirt,
corduroy shorts,
striped tube socks and cowboy boots
at the age of 2,

hook sliding my "green machine" big wheel under the street lights
before running into the house to watch "Dukes of Hazzard" on Fri-
day nights.
Intoxicated by the smell of my father frying catfish
with Hall & Oates
"Your Kiss is on My List"
swimming around in my head.
Always. Thinking. About. Girls.
The gift and the curse,
always around them
but it was always at church.
It didn't matter much anyway
because when it came to girls, I never knew what to say,
never knew how to say it,
but displayed it
like a young Forrest Gump...
clumsy and mute
which some girls found cute
behavior
but they didn't tell me about it until 15 years later!
Meanwhile,
I would call up the radio station
and do song dedications
for girls who never knew I existed.
"I Miss You" by Klymaxx
and "One More Night" by Phil Collins
were called in 1985
just before I turned 9,
right around the time
we were threatened by Hurricane Elena,
a short while later
my principal in elementary school
came into our classroom

to share the news
that the Space Shuttle Challenger exploded,
which reinforced my fear of death.
So I engulfed myself in music
used it to compensate for my lack of self-esteem and social skills
still proud of the fact
that I was a teenager during both of the golden eras of rap,
'87-'89,
'92-'95,
from Big Daddy Kane,
to G-thang,
from Poison Clan
to Redman,
from EPMD
to Steady B, Cool C, & EST,
stayed up late to watch Yo! MTV
but was lost
rockin a rayon shirt, S-curl, African medallion, and Travel Fox
that I copped from Soul Train,
along with a T-shirt with the airbrushed name
on the back,
humiliated because apparently I should've been good in basketball
just because I was black,
or so thought my classmates at private school,
increasingly suicidal and reclusive…until I discovered another tool
in 1989.
…assigned to start a personal journal
by my English teacher,
but to me…it sounded like a diary,
and dudes didn't do that,
unless you wanted to be considered gay or it affected your grade,
so for two weeks straight…I stared at a page
unable to lie my way through,

so I decided to write the truth,
no holds barred
no regard for my self-fabricated reputation
that I hated myself for faking,
and through my words
an unexpected, suppressed poet emerged,
fueled by isolation, hormonal imbalance, & "Straight Outta Compton"
by NWA,
took my first alcoholic drink between 9th & 10th grade
after watching Boyz II Men on stage
at Busch Gardens...
just before starting Hillsborough High School in '91,
rap was getting less fun
because it was becoming more about the money
than the message,
but I still bought tapes from Musicland every other weekend,
snuck in the movies to see "Juice" at Eastlake Mall,
didn't take my sophomore year in high school seriously at all
until I went to an end-of-the-year academic awards banquet... and
my name wasn't called.
I went home disgusted with myself,
listened to Nirvana
and A Tribe Called Quest
for hours,
I was
15.
...didn't know who I was
or who I wanted to be,
I just knew I wanted to be somebody
well-known,
or at the very least
have a report card that I could be proud to take home,
so I made a promise to myself on that day

that I was going to make better grades,
and for the next 2 years or
eight 9 weeks
I never made anything less than a "C",
and by 1993
I was convinced that I could go to college for free,
shocked when I found out that there were actually some girls
that were attracted to me,
Wow.
…anyway,
I traded in my beige church van
and headed off to FAM
in the Fall of '94:
Biggie, Snoop, Outkast, Wu-Tang Clan, Scarface, and Craig Mack
were killing rap,
Some East Coast cats
turned me on to Nas,
my people from Alabama and Louisiana introduced
me to Juvenile, Mystikal, 8-Ball & MJG,
I was one of the top cadets in ROTC
but my love for alcohol would come back to haunt me,
good student though,
faithfully went to class
but also partied during the week,
then to the Waffle House or Guthries to eat
which made it harder to get up for PT:
physical training,
same when
it came down to going to church,
first heard "Hit 'Em Up" at Gumbay in the summer of '96
about 3 months before Pac died,
found out B.I. was killed in a drive-by
the Sunday before our Spring Break in '97,

left in June of that same year for military advance camp out West
and I failed the physical fitness test,
lost my scholarship,
lost my future career as an officer in the US Army
as I recalled all the warnings
I ignored,
too ashamed to seek the Lord
but I did it anyway,
long story short…He allowed me to graduate Cum Laude
in '98,
almost 22 years to the date
of my birth,
at that time
Lauryn Hill was the most popular black woman on earth,
yeah…even more popular than Oprah
and instead of me becoming a soldier
I sold insurance for Allstate,
struggled trying to find my way
as a college grad,
back and forth between Tallahassee and Tampa
because I was in love
and it didn't cost so much to get gas,
fast forward to December 30, 2006,
30 years gone by quick
but not so fast that I can't remember…
remember how when me and my wife were dating each other,
we would put love songs on tapes and send them to one another,
remember how in the middle of our wedding,
the DJ played "Your Love Is a 187",
remember how my daughter was born on January 15, 2003
and we
watched the Bucs win the Super Bowl
and now we call it "the day hell froze",

yes,

the years have gone by quick,

but not so swift that I can forget the moments…and the music

the valleys that it seemed I would never come out of

and peaks that I tried to make last forever

like Keith's first record,

the mistakes that put me in spiritual and physical debt

yet

Christ paid it all,

still stumble and fall

sometimes,

but I'm slowly

…getting my legs under me,

bounce back like the original Rubberband Man

that I am,

with no 24's or a hustle that's grand,

just a plan to reflect on those pivotal issues and plights

that caused me to write,

and all the songs and the stories…

that make up the soundtrack…

of my life.

written by Walter 'Wally-B' Jennings

MAIN STREET

Southern Grits couldn't stick
A story so raw and rich.
The Steeles, McKinneys, and Smiths
were destined to click.

A Divine appointment
A resilience story.
A miracle manifest
A rise toward humility and God's glory.

Maine Street
A thoroughfare and primary district.
A birds-eye view and grassroots-sweet
She is so close…but distant.

The main attraction
She is fine as wine but hard to reach.
To Get to know her
Patience, time, and inquiry must speak.

Baby Maine
gained emotional weight that day.
Rotten wood floors
cradled bedtime baby blankets.

No lullabies, glass bottles
Or cribs.
No daddy's little princess
Innocent kisses or bibs.

Abandoned houses
Swaddled innocence.
Island Rum Alcohol perfume
coddled hospital rooms like incense.

Common.
But nonsense lingered.

Mental hospitals
Postpartum depression.
Poverty-stricken
No healthcare or native tongues.

Underdeveloped.
Lungs and breath released.

Separation anxiety between
Newborn baby and mum.
But love was winning
Light was shining.

Jamaican-American dreams were deferred
But hope was blue mountain climbing.
Citizenship thieves curbed enthusiasm
Dropped Balls with Plans unwinding.

House rentals drowning
In foreclosures.
A recipe for homelessness and
Schizophrenia paranoia.

But love was watching
Protecting and clocking.

One reunification dinner 18 years past time
Brought 5 siblings minus 1 in line.

Evidence of what God can do
Trampling Voodoo revealing truth.
A symbolic bridge over troubled waters
A community of sons and daughters.

A chef
Peacefully cooking in 5-star hospitality.
A contractor
Fighting to rebuild dream houses never made home.

A junior, passionate and erratic
An academic and black history fanatic.
Whose adopted mother lost her battle to soar
Cancer consumed…but she won the war.

A Spanish teacher
Breaking barriers and stereotypes.
Goals to defeat Autism
Searching for lost big sister prototypes.

First-generation American siblings conquering
Posting signs to confidently seek
A missing sister
Unsure of which state or city to peek.

It is impossible to learn
Priceless life lessons.
Preparation is real experience
Undiscovered university classes or sessions.
GEDs…community college

Diplomas and vocations.
Student loans, grief, forgiveness
Marriage and divorce in rotation.

What conquers darkness?
Who guarantees a victorious fight?

The designer of ten zillion towns
The journey navigator of the lost to found.
The lyricist of the word, 'Family'
Owner of the rights to understand me.

The atlas of my heart
The exceptional washer of feet.
He is the Alpha and Omega
The architect of Maine Street.

The heartland
That's heart-filled.
A poetic force
Made of organic Steele.

written by Charmaine
'C-Jennings' Maine

⌘

CHAPTER TWO
College, Camo, & Cold-Blooded Murder

Once you reach the milestone of becoming a young adult, excitement, anticipation, and confidence can overflow. Freedom is on the horizon. This is the moment when you either choose to activate, develop, and/or refine your morals and values or you become reactive and fall into the fly-or-die baby bird test. We all have choices and some of the first slips, falls and recoveries are not what you, your family, or your community could ever imagine. The key is to get up, own your choices, and ask yourself: Is who you are in alignment with your actions? Will your decisions change the trajectory of future outcomes?

Walter
Charmaine and I ended up going to college together after being in a long-distance relationship for eight months. I was so excited for her to come to Tallahassee, Florida. We both were finally going to be students at Florida A&M University, a famous historically black college/university (i.e. HBCU).

Charmaine, how did you feel about going to college to be with me? LOL.

Charmaine
Here we go! Uhhh...I went to college to get a degree not because of you buddy.

Walter
Okay. I think we both know the truth. LOL. Whatever you wanna tell yourself.

Charmaine
But seriously, I was excited to go to Florida A&M University. My FAMU HBCU college experience mirrored the 90s sitcom, A Different

World. University academia allowed me to grow in resilience and to develop as a scholar. I was blessed with a scholarship and welcomed with open arms by the local West Palm Beach FAMU alumni association. It was a bonus for us to be on the same campus after eight months of writing letters, creating music cassette tapes, and long-distance phone calls. Art was a major part of our relationship from the start. We would share our poetry either on the phone or in our letters. The mix tapes were epic because they often communicated intense emotions that we were often too shy to express out loud.

Walter

I was a business economics major. One of the things that was a big part of my college experience was being in the Army ROTC program. I was on a scholarship, which took a lot of my time. I did pretty well as it relates to ROTC leadership; however, I ran into problems when it came to meeting the physical expectations. The requirements to exercise and be disciplined in my nutrition and diet were an issue. A lot of the partying side of college caught up to me. In my later years, when it came to drinking and smoking, early morning physical training workouts became impossible to get up and honor on Mondays, Wednesdays, and Fridays.

Charmaine

Do you remember sending me pictures of you dressed in your ROTC uniform? Classic.

It meant a lot to me that you would freely share your heart. Especially the critical moments and hardships with ROTC. You were in a tough place, and I wasn't sure how to support you, other than to offer an empathetic ear to listen.

Walter, what did you need the most during that experience?

Walter

Well…my future was uncertain. I didn't know what was ahead. I knew that between your junior and senior years, you have to attend what's called advanced camp. The goal was to pass my advanced camp experience, graduate from college, and enter into the military as an officer. To do that, I needed to perform well at advanced camp. There is a six-week ROTC course and a portion focused on the physical fitness test.

Before you came to college, I went to camp and failed the physical fitness test. I got sent home, which meant that I was in danger of losing my ROTC scholarship. I was at risk of losing my potential career in the military and was completely devastated. I was suicidal and extremely embarrassed. I was depressed and my parents were adamant about me getting into summer school. It was a great decision and plan B. I didn't need to sit around, sulk, and grieve over it. I needed to get active and remember that the purpose of going to school was to get a degree. Eventually, I got back on track, enrolled in summer school, and applied for and secured a job at a local car dealership. Having you come to Tallahassee just a few months after that low point in my life really helped. It did my heart good, at least for a while.

Charmaine, what did you like about me, especially since I had several red flags according to your inferences?

Charmaine

Well…what I loved about you was that you showed vulnerability the first day that we met. That weekend you wrote me a letter. You were transparent about your experiences. You talked a lot and shared your genuine feelings. I felt very connected like we had been friends for a lifetime. A few months later, we kept calling and writing letters. The months were tedious, but we were persistent in making our long-distance relationship work. We didn't have cell phones, so it required effort to buy calling cards and coordinate talk times without the internet. You had limited access to money as a college student which was the same for me as a high school senior. You didn't pull back during the hardships. You let me in and expressed the struggles, which increased our level of emotional intimacy. It helped me to understand how I could support and encourage you. I felt safe with you and chose not to take the privilege lightly.

Walter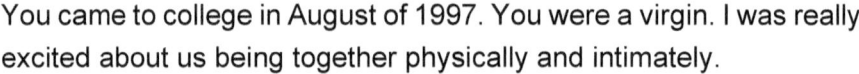

You came to college in August of 1997. You were a virgin. I was really excited about us being together physically and intimately.

What was it like being physically intimate for the first time after months of developing our relationship?

Charmaine

I was in love and excited to be around you. My hormones were raging but I was also scared to go against everything that I was taught. Excitement from both of us didn't lead us to have an intentional conversation about sex. We didn't make space to discuss what we thought it should look, feel, or sound like. We just flowed and I got caught up in the fairytale fantasy not thinking about potential consequences.

Walter

Yeah, I definitely wasn't thinking about the consequences. I was excited about you being in Tallahassee and taking our relationship to the next level. The last thing that crossed my mind was us getting pregnant or having a baby. I still remember when I took you to the clinic and the night before your test, you used the restroom pretty frequently. In my mind, I already kind of knew what the results would be. When you went to the clinic and then came back out to the car, and said, "I'm pregnant" - it was really tough because I didn't know what to do or how to respond.

Charmaine

I was scared, afraid, terrified, and desperate all at the same time. To me, this was the story that every parent fears will happen to their little girl. I believed that God was shining a light on me. I had to decide who I wanted to be, how I was going to behave, and what would be my path forward. The truth was that I violated my morals and values. There was no excuse because I knew better. I understood the consequences and that the spiritual expectation was to abstain from sex until marriage.

I made a choice and now I had to accept the consequences. I chose to be with you, and I gave in to that desire. You were not living a life of abstinence before our relationship, so the weight of that choice wasn't the same. I was ashamed that I had disappointed my family. My intrusive thoughts were that I was going to burden them with my poor decisions. Unfortunately, I fell into the stigma of making more mistakes while trying to cover up the initial mistake.

Walter

Well...it's one thing for me to do something and bear the burden of what I've done. It's another thing for me to do something that impacts someone else, and they have to live with the result of my choices. Ironically, this happened after getting kicked out of Army ROTC. In my mind, all of these were the consequences of the person I had become over the years. In college, I was living my life in a way that was forsaking my values. I had stopped going to church and reading my bible. I began to stray away from my spiritual foundation and my principles.

Everything that happened was related to my spiritual disconnect. Unfortunately, you trusted me with a gift as precious as your virginity and I did not handle it the right way. I felt like putting you in the middle of this situation was horrible. I felt responsible for you and that I had let you down. It was painful to know that I disappointed you, your family, and my family. When we made the decision not to go forward with the pregnancy, it was a stark reminder that whatever decision we made was going to be crucial. We were going to have to live with our choice for the rest of our lives. Whether we decided to terminate or go forward with the pregnancy, the decision would reverberate throughout the rest of our lives in some way. It is important to make sure that you really think through the exact decision, the specific actions that you are considering taking, and the potential consequences before you leap.

Charmaine

I remember hearing the anonymous expression, "Sin takes you farther than you want to go, makes you pay more than you want to pay, and keeps you longer than you want to stay." When you find yourself in deep trouble and you desperately need to recover, the easiest thing is to set your focus on other people instead of looking in the mirror. I tried to take complete ownership. It is very easy to blame your partner when an internal or external crisis strikes. When things flipped upside down, I wanted to hold on to blame, shame, and an internal space of unworthiness.

A million thoughts flooded my mind. Who was I to become a mother so young? How could I be so disrespectful to my family and their sacrifices for my future? How could Walter be so experienced and yet so inexperienced when it came to being proactive and using protection? The wonderful thing about being organically introspective is that you always turn around and ask yourself the same questions. You always have a mirror in front of your own face. You get realigned and refocused on your work. You operate in equity every day all day. So I had to ask myself why didn't I make better choices? Why didn't I hold myself responsible for securing, managing, and maintaining birth control? Why was I surprised by the outcome of my private sin being exposed?

This situation was the result of my free will, decision-making, and un-wise planning and preparation that led to this somber moment. I was on a fast rollercoaster ride to uncover what it truly meant to love. I was being challenged to look inward, live in alignment, and forgive with intensity. I was going to truly understand the power of God's love, Judas' panic and desperation, and Jesus' sacrifice on the cross. All of these things manifested in my heart as I came to the end of myself.

Walter
How did you recover and process your pain, guilt, and shame?

Charmaine
I took ownership, responsibility, and accountability for each choice. I had to celebrate the good choices and spend more time auditing the bad ones. I had to become an astute scholar of my behavioral health. I had to go through the grief cycle and accept who I became when my secrets were exposed. Acknowledging my ugly truth was the only way to begin the work of asking God to help me transform and change. We both fastened our seatbelts and entered a ride that quickly taught us what happens when you violate your morals and values. This bat-tle was brutal and taught us the dangers of self-abandonment and betraying God. It resulted in a full-blown identity crisis.
The recovery process is a critical time. It may be hard to look in the mirror and see your reflection. You learn about areas of yourself that are unattractive. It is hard to face for most people, but necessary. According to Dr. Phil, "We can't fix what we won't acknowledge."

Walter

Thank God for redemption. Redemption is always possible. Always.

RED FLAGS: LOVE IMPOSSIBLE

Red flags are unique gifts
Fantasy and reality sort and shift.
Forcing you to "green" inspect
Forcing you to "red" reflect.

Red flags make waves
But precious time they save.
They ask...What will you do with multiple options?
Will you accept red conflicts or drop them?

Which will you choose?
How hard will you love?
Will you select green or leave red ones?
Or all of the above?

Red flags are warning signs
They peek and hide.
Tease and taunt
Smokescreen, manipulate, and blindside.

They raise their sails
In high turbulent winds.
Gaslight, deny, deflect
Delay, haw, and hem.

When red flags are at bay
Be ready and prepared.
Guard your heart
Unapologetically or scared.
Your heart will say, "thank you" in advance.

written by Charmaine 'C-Maine" Jennings

RED FLAG SURVEY

Red flags are used as a sign of warning or danger. In relationships, some things are often said yet ignored. Green flags in relationships are indicators that reflect healthy emotional habits and genuine compatibility. Has someone ever said something that you believed could be a threat to themselves or the relationship? Read the list of statements and identify if you believe that the statement serves as a red flag (A) or green flag (B).

1. I love you more than I love myself.
2. Love means never having to say you're sorry.
3. Love is blind.
4. I only have eyes for you.
5. Time will heal all wounds.
6. My soulmate will always understand me.
7. Your true love will love all of you.
8. Love requires you to both forgive and forget.
9. It's true love when we keep on pleasing each other.
10. I want happily-ever-after. I need the "fairytale fantasy."
11. Happy couples don't disagree.
12. Real love never fades.
13. True love lasts forever.
14. Having a baby will heal our relationship.
15. Love is easy.
16. Words are enough.
17. Trust your feelings.
18. Compromise is key.
19. I can't live my life without you.
20. You complete me.

I USED TO LOVE HIM

The man that said he couldn't dance
But 2-stepped with me whenever given a chance.
Fashion like Boys-II-Men
Meets The Temptations precision.

Clean-cut and styled to the bone
Reps his city and loves his home.
Proud to come from The West
Just around the corner from the projects.

Head held high with pride
No matter falling down by the wayside.
His college degree conferred, but with no money, no food
Humility fueled His work in a labor pool.

I used to love him.

His opinions deemed my fashion decisions, 'comfy but off.'
Like Queen Latifah in "Set It Off"
I wore navy blue Dickie suits
Black steel toe boots

Blue grandma-knitted sweaters
Like scratched records to long-distance love letters.
My make-up was sporting a summer head cold
Toilet tissue in hand to wipe my snotty nose.

Tore up from the floor-up
Florida's bottom up is where our origin story spills.
Our romance catapulted up

On top of the highest of seven hills.

Tallahassee Florida
Advancing our knowledge and life skills.
At Florida A&M University
Where everyone could see.

Does your girlfriend have advanced stages of Cataracts?
Or is LOVE truly blind?
Man, come on! How can she be COLD?
When it's 102° degrees outside?!

I used to love him.
The love of my life
Would fight to preserve Date Night.
Regular 1998 visits to a Vinyl Fever music store
A harsh reminder that he and I were college-poor.

Prepared to sell his best CDs
While the store clerk looks at him crazy.
"Man...You gon sell Jay-Z, Donell Jones, and Biggie
Outkast, and Tupac's Machiavelli?

Comments that fell on deaf ears
His mind was set on VHS Movies from BlockBuster.
The Winn-Dixie grocery store seafood section
For four-dollar per pound crab leg clusters.

No high blood pressure or cholesterol worries
Just Old Bay seasoning, extra butter, and garlic.
We were Ride or Die friends
Committed to finishing what we started.

I used to love him.
A blessing to his friends and family
Strangers benefitted from his experience.
Gave his all in all things
Saw the best of the best in others' DREAMS.

Achieved his GOALS
a sight unseen.
He spent 8 1⁄2 years between…
High school and college ROTC.

Military missed calls,
Disappointment, tumbles, and falls.
Bad decisions and Mistakes,
Pain, hurt, and heartbreaks.

I used to love him.
To people of the light
No one gets life perfectly RIGHT.
That's why I loved him
But not as much as the heavenly Him.

Never my judge
Required me to grow.
Told me about myself
And things I didn't know.

Helped me love myself more
Only then could I appreciate and ADORE
the earthly HIM.
My friend
my husband.

The guy who couldn't dance
But 2-stepped with me whenever given a chance.
Head held high with pride
No matter how his future wife looked by his side.

The love of my life
Who still fights to preserve date night.
The man with a calling on his life
A passion for spoken word
Devotion to Christ
Advocate for TEEN Voices UnHEARD
A hard-working father, husband, and son who serves.

I used to love him.
But now...
I truly love the God-Spirit within.

written by Charmaine 'C-Maine' Jennings

STUCK IN MY HEAD

Our paths should have never crossed.

I was lost on a never-ending search for true love,
but the truth was
I was pretty content with not finding it.

You?
Well, you did your own thing,
and would never let a man bring
more drama in your life.
Not with school and parents providing their fair share,
and I guess…that's where God comes in.

Only God could have given me the insight,
the light to notice you
after accidentally ignoring you all night.

Only God could have given you that swagger,
I was feeling somebody else, but you were badder,
and it wasn't what you wore,
but how you rocked it,
had a spades game going on
but baby girl stopped it,
because when you walked in, all talking came to a complete halt,
and the first thing that popped in my mind was
"Man, look at how she walks!"
So, before we even assessed the situation,
"your walk" and I had a conversation.

...and "your walk" informed me that you were lonely,
but not looking,
and only the genuine in heart
could even get to know you past the walk.
So I took heed and agreed,
because this young lady had finesse,
and before she opened her mouth,
I was already impressed,
normally,
I would have been contemplating being undressed,
but not with you,
not with only a few days left before I was to return home.

I just wanted to know you,
to show you that my intentions were real,
so as we strolled the Atlantic
and times stood still,
I fell into your eyes.
...and while I was there, I danced with your emotions until we
kissed,
and we journeyed to a land where true love exists,
and if there was ever a case of love at first sight,
It happened that night.

Oftentimes...
I find myself watching you sleep.
I wonder if you can truly fathom the way we came to be.
The laws of nature and relationships that we manipulated
to make it.
I try not to disturb you
but quietly whisper that "I don't deserve you,"
and you answer by unconsciously rolling over,
while thoughts of our first date keep going over and over

to act as a reminder that now that I found The One,
the quest has only just begun.

written by Walter 'Wally-B' Jennings

BLOODY MURDER

According to TD Jakes...
"Nobody can comfort you like someone who has seen
God dig them out of a ditch!"

Experience plus Confession is good for the soul,
Who will admit the switch?

Have you ever been... Lost?
Whipped?
Knocked down?
Kicked?

A prisoner or A patient?
Recruited by the evil agent... of death?

Who lies and speaks his native tongue.
He wraps the 20% lie
into 80% truth
To confuse and twist tongues

Have you ever killed someone,
With your Thoughts? Words? or Hands?
Are you the first to come in last,
Are you the present or your dark past?

Does your secret closet hide skeleton bones misbehaving?
Is a murderer's life worth ending... or saving?

There is a bloody stained hospital gown,
No doctors or nurses are around

Just the evidence of a crime scene.
A vital signs monitor that once upon a time beeped

It now screeches a soprano high-pitched note
The vital waves, now wave goodbye
As flatlines take over.
Over and out for the count,

Number One
A high school girl meets college guy.
Moonlight kisses awaken a long-distance romance.
They fall in love.
After eight months
They are free to be together.
They become one.

But Number Two happened.
Literally.
They became a wet hospital floor.
Without the yellow sign
A slip and fall accident that placed her neck and soul on the line.
Poor choices and bad decisions multiplied.
No lawsuits were filed... although spiritual laws were broken.
Her third month in college and she had already lost focus.

Three,
A college dropout, A family disappointment,
Unwed and questioning,
If their love and love seed were worth it?
How could she rewind the hands of time?

Number Four

Forewarns us that sin will take you farther than you want to go,
Keep you longer than you want to stay,
Cost you more than you could ever afford to pay.
She and the guy she thought she loved
Fought for their current dreams
Which didn't include college dropouts, diapers, and wedding rings

They plotted the murder of a child,
Abandoned responsibility.
Immediately remembering how she judged "that" girl in high school
Who in four years had three.

Now the "ticking clock" is her judge,
Prepared to sentence her to death or life without parole,
Her mind, Her body, and Her soul,
Were all conflicted.

Five
It was hard to look in the mirror
At the contradiction she had become.
In high school she professed,
And promised to "never" do anything like this.
She was once considered a Saint
Now a cold-blooded Judas!

Just like "him" she wanted to sin again
Guilt-filled and riddled with shame
She wanted to take her life
Move far away and change her name

How could God use her filth to foster someone else's purity?
To use that which is dirty to make others clean?
She didn't mean for any of this to happen, but it did.

Six,
She picked up a piece of paper and pen
Drafted a suicide letter
But the phone rang
A voice smothered in pain
Vulnerable and marked with a life-or-death decision
Was haunted by a loud tick-tock clock stalking and preparing a similar sentence.

Three more phone calls came within the weeks that followed.
She became their clergy and their wise spiritual counsel.
She had no time to wallow in her bloody mess.
Her creator rejected her suicide letter in protest.

Seven,
The "one" life she took would be the only one
The compelling words of her transparent testimony and tongue
Would save 4 young women and 4 unborn babies.
Nothing is ever lost.
Forgiveness and redemption always come at an expensive cost
Too high for anyone to actually pay.

Eight,
She rededicated her life to Christ.
The only blood sacrifice that could break her chains
Free her from her prison cell
Make her actually forgive herself and...
To Believe the encouragement she offers to Everyone Else

Nine,
Forgiven she needed to say goodbye
To attend the funeral of her young immature mind

To sit in the seat of accountability
To acknowledge that she didn't know what she didn't know
But She NOW knows to "Judge not lest ye be judged and....
Never say Never!"

Ten,
She placed a single red rose in the open casket and closed the lid,
Promised to waste no more tears
For the bad decisions of an erased past
Immediately tested,
The usher and only other person at the funeral asked...
"Are you and the deceased related, you look like twins,
She is so young? Are you her close friend?"

The new version of the young woman replied,
She is a distant memory
That girl was my bloody hospital gown
Evidence of a crime scene
Her red hands and young mind
Couldn't handle her own controversy

You asked, "Who was she?"
She was a scared young girl.
She taught me to only look in the mirror
After asking God first, what He sees

She taught me that I have permission
To wear a royal robe of reconciliation
That my hands are clean and ready
To be crowned with authority

She taught me about the person I DO and do NOT want to be

In her death, she introduced me to King David, Moses, and The Apostle Paul
To visit the beauty of their graves and ashes
To study their scandals, restoration, and passions

Most importantly…
That they and I no longer have a secret closet with skeleton bones misbehaving!
She taught me that a murderer's life "is" actually worth saving

written by Charmaine 'C-Maine' Jennings

⌘

CHAPTER THREE
The Wedding Of A Lifetime...Or Not

Charmaine

When I was a little child, I loved weddings. I loved the entire process so much that my first birthday gift confirmed this passion. My amazing parents took me to Toys "R" Us and allowed me to pick out any present that I wanted. Correction. Any present within the budget. Lol. The perfect gift appeared when my seven-year-old eyes connected with, "The Wedding Bears." Two white furry bride and groom bears dressed in a tuxedo and a wedding dress with a veil. The blushing bride wore a tiara with rose-colored cheeks. They were happy and they had Velcro on their paws, which meant they had a bond. They would stick together forever. They represented love, unity, and family.

My dream wedding included those exact ingredients. I desired a winter-themed wedding in the great Sunshine state. Yeah. Yeah. Okay?! I know it sounds like a contradiction, but it was "my" dream…alright?! A Christmas wedding is a more appropriate description of the experience since it's only a cool breeze in Florida to most northerners. I loved the lights, Christmas tree smells, and the festive mood of the holiday season overall. Not only did I want my wedding decorated in lights, but I also loved the way my hometown, West Palm Beach glimmered with holiday cheer. I envisioned my dad walking me down the aisle in my childhood church, Antioch Missionary Baptist. I envisioned everyone standing as I walked toward my future husband and life partner. The day would be smooth, peaceful, and seamless. It was literally going to happen like the many pre-tend weddings that I planned for my wedding bears.

Dreams are amazing and necessary, but let's get to what really happened. The wedding of a lifetime was more like… "the hardest work of a lifetime." If Rihanna was a journalist, she would have reported that our wedding was… "hard work, work, work, work, work, work" to the tenth power. Leading up to the wedding, there were so many things to think about. My mom and I were essentially the wedding planners. Well, she was the mastermind. The clock was ticking, and people still needed to be invited to be in our bridal court. We needed to create a guest list and the program logistics needed to be established. My mom is a fantastic seamstress, so she made my dress. It had a crystal-beaded bodice and a French chiffon 3-foot train skirt. As a result, my parent's living room looked like a fashion showroom exploded and a print factory shut down in the middle of program printing. Yikes!!! She had a lot on her plate. She also made the bridesmaids dresses and designed the programs. The bridesmaids were called in for emergency duty to help finish the programs. Wow... this was a full-blown production! There were so many decisions to make, conversations, invitations, and disappointments from people who desired to be in the wedding court and/or involved in some way. Uncomfortable, but a good problem to have. The planning process can be a huge distraction. The details seemed less about the person I was preparing to spend my life with and more about which of our guests desired to eat fried chicken, baked chicken, or holiday ham? Who wants collard greens and needs a salad? Which bridesmaids preferred off-the-shoulder dresses or block-heeled shoes?

Fast forward. After months of planning, our wedding day was finally here. I arrived at the church super-duper late. I was exhausted from my Bachelorette party the night before. My energy was low because I only had 3 hours of sleep. I felt the stress of people waiting on me and the inconvenience of their time. My mother told me as I put my veil on to remember that my fiancé was still young. She warned me that he, like most men, would need time to mature before becoming a solid husband. Bad timing mom!!!!! I didn't want to hear that, but OMG... after years of marriage, I had to admit that she was so very right!!! #ListenToMarriedOGs

When I was finally dressed and ready to walk down the aisle, I waited for everyone to stand up. I was thinking Yes!!!! This is the moment in my wedding dream. Unfortunately, three or four incorrect songs played before the correct bridal march played. It was almost like a comedy show. Will they get the right CD track? Maybe this time! No. Okay.. the next one. OMG. Which song will they play next? We began to hear the lyrics, "Your Love Is A 187." Really??? If this song was foreshadowing for our relationship, we were in serious trouble. Details matter and no one told the coordinator which CD track on the album actually marked the spot. She was amazing and very supportive. I became overwhelmingly nervous. At that moment, I didn't want people staring at me. Ouch!!! It may sound crazy because most people don't know that I have extreme spotlight nerves. I defaulted back to my shy demeanor not wanting the attention portrayed in my original dream. I took a deep breath to calm my nerves.

Once the Whitehead Bros song, "Beautiful Black Princess" started to play… I looked at my dad, he smiled, and we walked to the front of the church. My pastor, fiancé, and his big brother and best man each seemed happy and a little nervous too. The pastor confirmed that he was really really nervous judging by the beads of sweat on his forehead. He admitted that this was his first wedding. During the ceremony, he set such high expectations for himself that he could barely get our names correct. After several attempts on December 30, 2000, he married Walter Winters and Trameka Smith. To this day, we don't know who those two people are but years later we were happy to make history as his first couple. On the other hand, my sister, who was also the maid of honor, quickly objected to the pastor's name attempts because her name is Tamiko Smith, and it was too close for comfort. Years later I still tease her that "she" may be the one actually married to a guy named Walter Winters somewhere in North America.

The wedding was fun, family-oriented, and a representation of life ahead. Imperfect, spontaneous and made pleasant when you have God, family, and support. Everything that could go wrong did, but we looked back on our wedding day and gained some great stories because we made it our intimate comedy festival. No, it wasn't perfect...but it will definitely be a permanent memory of laughs, bloopers, and things to remember. My husband had a pretty adventurous night before the wedding as well, but we will save that for another book. After the ceremony and reception, we rode off into the sunset in a white Rose Royce vintage car. We were happy to leave the wedding event/process behind. We appreciated our loved ones, family, and friends, but we really, really needed to sleep. The next day we prepared for our honeymoon adventure with Bahama sunsets, carnival parades and quiet time together. In conclusion, this was the story of a lifelong wedding dream turned into reality...or not. The end.

MISPLACED EMOTION

The word love is just that- a word.
A verb because it requires action.
Something set into rotation until it has your heart racing.
Yet some of us never even get out of the blocks
because we're blocked,
which leads us to be confused on what love is and is not.

…and I was one of those for a long time.
I always used the wrong line,
on the wrong dime,
because I was scared to speak from my own mind.
I looked,
read books on what a girl wants,
what a girl needs,
but then it occurred to me that maybe I was aiming too high,
because I had my eyes set on what I really wanted but I kept getting
hurt.
So I got to thinking that maybe that wasn't what I deserved.

I just wanted to matter
…to cause laughter
in the mouth and heart of someone that would see through me.
…through the less than stylish clothes,
through the van that I drove,
through my red eyes and mucus if I ever had a cold.
but…what did I have to offer?
I had no edge,
no ill whip,
no fresh kicks,

no game,
no name brand clothes,
so as my friends were picked and chose,
I was left outside as the getaway car,
and as I listened to the radio station,
I received a moment of revelation:
Maybe the reason why I didn't get any play
was because my heart always got in the way.

So sex became my motivation,
but again my heart would always intervene,
and while I was in her jeans
I left a part of myself and gained nothing from her,
so I walked away from those encounters feeling emptier
...and I searched for love,
but didn't know what it was,
what it looked like,
where to look at.
thinking Love=A Girl + A Sex Act
and if I hit it just right then maybe she just might...
So when love finally came and called my name,
I failed to realize the prize
that had fallen before my eyes
and I did her wrong.

My second love.
...but I didn't realize it until 2 weeks after we broke up,
wonder why I was choked up,
I thought it was the two years down the drain.
The pain,
the rain we had walked through hand in hand,
more than a lover I had lost a best friend.
and more than being friends,

we lost a child,

and while I lived in denial,

she lived in hopes that I wouldn't misconstrue the magnitude of what had happened,

take us more seriously,

but mysteriously it totally flew over my head that all she wanted was me.

So things fell apart and I was left with the pieces,

the reasons why I lost what I feverishly sought,

And after all the hurt and anger,

I recognized it was my fault.

…and I cried.

I cried myself to sleep,

and my mother begged for me to eat.

Then the secret of love that was concealed,

Had been revealed,

consumed and moved me like the Holy Spirit,

my mind, body, and soul bared witness,

and I looked into a mirror...

and it wasn't what I saw

but how I saw it,

spotted,

the love that I looked for in others,

in the backseat of jeeps and under bedroom covers,

then my eyes begin to swell,

as I thought of the hell,

I put myself through to find The One,

but now that I had spun,

I found myself in the exact position where I had begun,

I thought of the lies that I had told,

daughters' hearts I had stole,

scene after scene of saying things I didn't mean!

and I faced that mirror…

all alone…

and it pierced me like a high-pitched tone…

I had finally seen the person…

I should have loved all along.

written by Walter 'Wally-B' Jennings

I DON'T NEED A DIAMOND, I AM ONE

Ask yourself if buying an expensive ring...
Is a court jester of vanity or your ego's wings?
Is it a symbolic circle of love, peace, and harmony...
Or slave mentality plus capitalism equals American greed?

Do not pressure to buy
Or buy under pressure
If this is a means to an end
It will be the end of your means.
No ultimatums.

The stronger the pressure,
The brighter my shine.
Why do men desire my treasure,
But fail to mine-minds?

How deep is their being?
And how deep will they go?
How dare they ask for strength?
But get angered when equally yoked?

I DON'T NEED A DIAMOND, I AM ONE!

Their mindsets expose will-sets and skill sets,
Void of context and substance.
I hoard my most valuable gems
I illuminate my genius,
I vow to honor only the man who leads with spirit, heart...
Not his penis.

I applaud selflessness, supportive and sensual superpowers,
I stand in ovation because he yields to the highest power.
A man who admits without God he is no one special,
No weapon formed against him will prosper
Because God Almighty is his vessel.

I need love like God intended,
One knowledgeable of every hair on my head.
I need a patient, kind, and sacrificial love,
That quenches my mind so my spirit gets fed.

One who knows he can do all things through Christ
When he seeks ye first the kingdom,
One whose faith is lived out loud
And evidenced by his witness and wisdom.

I DON'T NEED A DIAMOND, I AM ONE!

I absolutely need a scalp massage
For no reason in the middle of the night.
I need a professional scholar
Prepared to study me for the rest of his life.

I need integrity to guide our finances
And maturity to manage his ego and mouth.
I need a man who will drive
6.5 hours to ask me out.

I need a poet man
Who can understand my metaphors and similes
A wordsmith that can scribe messages
only my soul can read.

I need a prodigy
To feed my intellect like I've been fasting for 40 days and nights.
I need a man so attentive
He can anticipate my sexual appetite.

It is always his pleasure to serve me
To master my body whether put together or in pieces.
A man who listens and is quiet
And can love me through all of the 5 senses.

I DON'T NEED A DIAMOND, I AM ONE!

I need a love with no expiration date
That comes with a lifetime guarantee
A life story that my great-great-grandchildren
will one day beg us to read

I need love letters and mixtapes
To fall asleep on the phone because no one wants to hang up
Eyes never too old to flirt and fantasize
And bottomless pineapple-lemonade frozen cups.

I DON'T NEED A DIAMOND, IF YOU ARE ONE!

I desire barefoot powder-white beaches.
I need swaying palm trees,
Holding hands…falling asleep on his chest
Under a moonlight sea breeze.

I need tender forehead kisses,
An intimate exchange of heart,
An unmatched work ethic,

Compassion for family and fine arts.

I DON'T NEED A DIAMOND, WHEN YOU ARE ONE!

I have a man who gets stronger under pressure,
His shine uniquely inspires the mind.
When he desires my treasure,
Never will he get his before I get mine.

I have a man who knows how to mine-minds.
How to succeed under pressure
His goes deep and his being is deep.
He's regimented and measured.

Bold, He asks for what he wants.
He gets down on bended knee
In public and in front of my family
Vowing to give the best love of my life in 360 degrees.

I DON'T NEED A DIAMOND, BECAUSE I HAVE ONE!

written by Charmaine 'C-Maine' Jennings

PRE-NUPTIAL DISAGREEMENT

"Dearly beloved...
Families and Mothers...
We are here before God and the company of others,
to join these two in holy matrimony..."
Is this what I want?
I hope I wasn't just lonely.

We were apart for a month,
and I missed her so much,
but was that Love or Lust?
Fear or Trust?
Let me think through this because there is no "I" in "Us".

The way this preacher is talking forever seems so long,
how many people I said forever to are so far gone,
but this commitment is eternal,
I'll be joined at the Spirit,
women will see my wedding ring and won't want to come near it,
no more coming in late,
or leaving the house after 3:00,
and before long,
I'll be learning how to put in car seats!

Look at all my boys laughing,
they know what's about to happen,
no more hanging out at the club,
late night so-called macking,
my mind says I'm crazy,
my heart won't compromise,

one look at my bride's eyes,
this decision I'll never despise,
how often does something perfect fall right on your doorstep?
Letting this good thing go is the only thing I regret.

That's why the carat-and-a-half
was worth me not getting a Nav,
I may still drive a Honda,
but I'm marrying a Jag!

What in the world was I thinking?!
This is the perfect woman for me,
…but when she thought about her future plans,
am I the person she thought it would be?
I mean…I snore a little bit,
I'm kind of overweight,
but I don't want my imperfections to mean that I can be replaced,

"…to have and to hold…"
Pastor, hell no!
I won't say it out loud
but I'm thinking it in my soul.

…before I knew it,
300 people heard me say "I Do",
felt like a prison door closing,
"Cell Block 22!"

"I now pronounce you two husband and wife",
either my stomach won't stop churning or this tux is too tight,
but when I kissed my bride,
it felt like the first time,
and I may not know what I'm getting into,

but at least I know it's all mine.

written by Walter 'Wally-B' Jennings

⌘

CHAPTER FOUR
Marriage For Dummies: Young, Dumb, & In Love!

Walter

Alright so...we got married when I was 23 years old, and Charmaine was 21 years old. We were educated and received our college degrees first. We both came from two-parent homes. Charmaine's parents are married and now have been for over 50 years. My parents are also together and they have been married for over 60 years. We were confident that not only was our marriage going to be rock solid, we absolutely positively did not need premarital counseling. Besides, we had everything that we needed inside of us in order to have a great marriage...or so we thought. It is unknown by most people that Charmaine & I were officially married at the Leon County courthouse on March 16, 2000. The day we decided to marry was to honor God with our relationship. After the ceremony, we got into a huge argument. We were literally in the car leaving the courthouse and entered into the worst argument of our entire relationship. We were not that couple that argued...so why now? To this day I don't even know what the argument was about.

Charmaine

My first thoughts after the argument while leaving the courthouse was maybe we should have opted to invest in premarital counseling and received the marriage license discount on the back end. It wasn't about the money. Clearly the county clerk's office knew something that we did not. People who make the investment to set themselves up for success reap the reward because they are intentional. They are proactive in preparing for the wonderful, good, bad, and ugly. My many first thoughts after the argument when the car went silent was – "What did I do?" I just ruined my life. I don't even know who he is right now. Of course, I knew him! Or did I? We had been dating for a total of four years. Why am I questioning what I heard from the Lord?

WHAT WE LEARNED...

Four years of dating and we didn't even argue like this! We went from being completely happy, sure of ourselves, and knowing that this is who God told us we were supposed to marry…to that one argument planting a seed of doubt…just that fast.

So there were three things that over the years we've realized were really important in that moment, especially during the younger years of our marriage.

The first one is that everyone needs premarital counseling! Every marriage and relationship is unique and different, and you cannot base the success of your marriage on the credit score of your parents. Pre-marriage education is needed whether your parents divorced, or they have a wonderful marriage. Success isn't based on whether your parents were a good influence and/or they set the atmosphere for you to witness a great model. The good thing about individuals who come from a single-parent home or from divorced parents is that you are empowered to write your own story. You have a chance to actually create the marriage that you want. So, the first thing is that everybody needs premarital counseling.

The second one is that we uncovered that we have a cornerstone marriage. A cornerstone marriage is one where both individuals are actually building and growing together-individually and collectively. We were both very young. We were still getting to know ourselves. To be honest, we were discovering who we were and coming into the changes that we needed to make within. That was really critical for us to embrace the fact we needed to be patient with one another. Not just in our marriage, but in our individual life journeys.

There are benefits and there are some challenges to cornerstone marriages. One benefit was that while getting to know each other, we were building our finances, lives, and careers from the ground up. A cornerstone is the base, the foundational building block of any major building structure. Cornerstone marriages can be highly successful because you are building together, but there are some challenges as well. When couples are young, they are not fully developed. The marriage may be fragile or waver in focus. Morals and values may not be clearly established, managed, maintained, or communicated which may create conflict. Adjoining yourself to someone else before you confidently establish your individuality can cause long-term issues.

The third one is that we both learned to let go of our preconceived notions of marriage. Marriage is about service to your spouse rather than yourself. Your spouse should not serve you out of obligation, it is really about embracing the work. You are committing to a work that will have you punching the clock every single day. The Bible talks about renewing your mind and marriage, which is about reconfirming your commitment every single day.

Lastly, the challenge with cornerstone marriage is that it is easy to get comfortable. It's easy to say, well…this person knows me. Both of you have to do the work to individually evolve. The most important thing is to be your best self and ensure that the marriage is maturing. The way that you do that is by dating and continuing to invest in new ways to connect. It is a commitment to date one another for life. For example, when you get a promotion on the job or become parents, you don't get permission to stop dating your spouse. Our children have seen us date throughout their entire childhood and teenage years. Now that our eldest child is an adult, we want her to remember that we have modeled the key values and principles. Couples should demonstrate their beliefs by going out on dates, dressing up and continuing to invest into their relationship.

INCINERATING PERRY ELLIS SLACKS

I told the justice of the peace: "I Do."
The truth is…I thought I did.
I thought I was ready for forever.
I thought I was ready for one love,
with one person,
one song,
with one version,
I mean after 3 years of dating,
either you know or you don't,
and being a man
we never really know if we will or
we won't.
Play most things by ear,
play most girls through fear,
made plans to go there,
but ended up here,
well…I ended up here with doubts,
read books and thought I had marriage all figured out.

I told the justice of the peace: "I Do".
The truth is…I thought I did.
I thought I was ready for kids
and baby bibs
sterilizing nipples
and putting together cribs.
I look at what we have to offer each other
and the world is enough,
the funny thing about being offered the world is that it may be too
much,
at least right now,

most of my friends try to convince me not to,
argue that I will regret it,
I said, "not true".

I told the justice of the peace: "I Do".
The truth is…I thought I did.
I thought I knew,
thought I was ready for life with
only you
but when you get on my nerves,
I got to deal with it,
I can't just jump up and leave because you make me sick,
when you have a headache and don't feel like having sex,
I don't have some women on the side to relieve that stress,
in the middle of the game,
you want to turn the station,
and let's not talk about our temperature situation!
I'm always waking up sweating with a fever,
you got your electric blanket on and the heater?!
I try to keep the peace so some things I don't say,
I understand you're always cold but it's almost May!

I told the justice of the peace: "I Do."
The truth is…I thought I did.
I thought I could handle it,
bumps and bruises while we dated
we just bandaged it,
went on our merry way,
anxious to see each other
hurried quickly through our day! What happened?
Now I'm anxious to get away,

I told the justice of the peace I'd take you

in spirit and truth,
from rags to suits,
on bikes and coupes,
we're supposed to work through it, not "I" but a group,

I told the justice of the peace: "I Do",
but the truth is
I didn't know what "I Do" was,
But now…"I Do."

written by Walter 'Wally-B' Jennings

RINGS, DRESSES, & FONDANT DREAMS

It seems that dreams uprooted
Verbally expressed.
Impress upon the temporal lobe
To loathe replicas of reality.

You are asleep!

Objects, actions, and perceptions
Offer no objections.
To this revolutionary
hallucinatory experience.

This poem is rated, "Fantasy!"

Rings, dresses, and sweet gooey fondant cake
Can take 3-4 decades to create.
So why wait
When no one is getting younger.

Undercover,
In between sheets with random lovers.
Is not your buttercream flavor or filling
You fulfill the mind and tongue with mustard seeds.

So addicted you pop faith pills
Like top shelf pharmacy products
From pill mills
That recruit the ill skilled and high-willed

But question, will this dream come true?

Because you have wanted this
Before lipstick.
Before Training bras
Before puberty.

You desired a decadent wedding bliss
A romantic peppermint kiss.
Huge crinoline slips
A white dress and mosaic appliques.

They may stay on
But later come off.
When off duty brides
challenge eager grooms to rise and find
garter belts on curvy thighs
that cry out Sexual Healing by Marvin Gaye.

A handsome groom
Prepared to jump brooms
Must wipe his mouth from drool
Smitten by her essence

Flash Mobbing a teary eye
that rains at the perfect moment.
For she is the sight of majesty
Walking.
Almost floating in Queendom.

Heavy in heart
Enlightened by tender love,
humility

meek and made of steel

She is organically real
Ready to steady her hand.
Uncontrollably…her dad's hand begins to shake.

For the father is consumed
Too tough to admit this bridal march happened way too soon.
Just 20 years ago
She crowned from her mother's womb

Now Dad must bless the groom with her life
In humble sacrifice
Both promise to surrender the need to be right.
The need to win
The need to fight
The need to end the night angry about nothing and happy about
everything

Conquering the light of day
Celebrating sound
Unspeakable joy for everyone around
Everything round
Like the rings of matrimony
That Holy grips on tips of fingers that linger in awe of the iridescent
shine.

What's mine will be his
And what's his will be mine.
Like cake smashed in faces
We will tackle hardships from spiritual places

In public spaces with cameras, witnesses, and champagne toasts

Our life story will ultimately showcase
Whether we will serve and protect ourselves
or if we obey and trust God the most.

Together
Glasses cling
The crowd screams, cheers, and applauds
Crowding the dance floor to slide electric
Smiles and laughs abundant
Joy unspeakable
Flirty looks
Wedding bell kisses
Shiny rings
Puffy dresses
Sweet Reality
Sweet Fondant Dreams.

Girl!
Wake Up!!!!

written by Charmaine 'C-Maine' Jennings

PAINT BY NUMBERS

Ever since the beginning of time man has been fascinated with the
idea of playing GOD...
and every now and again the Most High will give us an opportunity to
prove how truly inadequate we are.
Fresh start.
Clean slate.
No excuses.
Just a blank canvas
and a million and one chances
to paint the portrait of perfection we dream about,
so we gradually pick our colors out
from an infinite spectrum...
we select them,
and then test them before they're added to our palate,
raw talent and hungry eyes behind each brush stroke
and every opportunity brings hope that...
this will be our masterpiece.

A definitive work that marks our legacy,
a silent awe that speaks for me
beauty...rarely needs an explanation,
visual tones cascading
within our spirit,
we remove the ceiling
of our coupes
and let our potential kiss the sky,
aim our patriot missiles high
and shoot down angels
that become our subjects,
our muse,

our own little piece of heaven in tunics and heeled shoes
this isn't love.
This is art.
Colorful.

So I tell her...
allow me to immortalize you
in hues
you kept hidden in the eyes of your adolescent dolls,
lower the drawbridge of your walls
so I can discover the majesty of your castle,
I come in peace,
bearing only the two arms GOD has given me
these are not lines,
this is a message from The Divine
to whom you've been praying,
the Boaz you requested now stands before you...waiting.
I begin painting...

...envelop her days with blue watercolor skies and pallid clouds
shaped like Jamaica,
in the afternoons I take her
on long walks where we cross
lavender and gold bridges,
we stop every couple of minutes
to skip rocks
and then walk barefoot through lush jaded fields,
all the while...she remains quiet and still,
the color of serenity,
fascinated by her energy
I smear her orange and burgundy evenings
and routinely
attempt to dazzle her with flashes of St. Elmo's fire,

gently tilt her head higher
and point out the stars
that were patterned after her eyes,
she wants to cry...
but I warn her that stardust
will only leave a trail behind,
we are 2nd grade Valentines
believing that life is as sweet as the candy we share:
Her-Twizzlers and Werther's.
Me-Butterfingers and Starburst
we make bets to see who will run out of words first,
...we usually tie,
our eyes
play hopscotch as we watch the edges of darkness neatly fold its corners
and tuck itself behind the horizon,
she is a yellow dawn rising
as if to say... "Good Morning".
Renewed mercy and grace...
her face
is the center of my solar system
which explains why her lips burn when I kiss them,
but this isn't love.
This is art.
Paint stains on my smock
in retrospect,
should've reminded me
that my hands are unsteady.
'Anxious' doesn't mean you're ready
I am green.
...still growing,
holding her innocence like judgment
standing before your honor,

she has disrobed her armor
and entrusted me with her beautifully broken vessel,
but what happens when you're more 'excited' than 'careful'?
When you decide to change the number sequence
and dismiss the lines you were supposed to stay within,
there are some laws...that not even GOD can bend
as sin stains red on the canvas,
apologies can't undo collateral damage
it only reinforces the voices you ignored,
potential drips on the floor
I am a deity with no ability
to stop tears and colors from running,
doing everything and nothing
fumbling towards ecstasy,
because ever since the beginning of time
man has been fascinated with the idea of being the Lord of Lords,
King of Kings,
only to end up as the Lord of a
3 Ring
T-Pain
Lupe Fiasco,
longing for a power we were born not to know,
standing at the foot of her rainbow
holding the colors of love
that no longer resemble the palate I selected,
and if I'm a God that cannot lie...how can broken promises be cor-
rected?
How can I mend her broken heart
without a fresh start?
A clean slate?
I heard 'em say only cowards run away from the messes they make...
but fools stay
believing they can somehow make amends,

these are the things that change boys to men
when we CAN run...but don't.
I used to be afraid that she would one day forget me...
Now I'm afraid she won't,
afraid she's no longer willing to pose for my rendering
but I can't seem to find a color...for 'forgiving',
can't blot out these sporadic shades of gray
that randomly appear
and it's now clear that...I'm no Picasso,
let alone God.
...and this isn't art.

This is love.

Flawed perfection.

A portrait of divine lessons
that only makes sense over time,
because we must learn to embrace the process,
so that we can truly appreciate the design.

written by Walter 'Wally-B' Jennings

⌘

CHAPTER FIVE
The Drama Of Trauma:
Liquor & Lick
Her Secrets

TRAUMA

A big impact that fits into tiny spaces.
A one-hit wonder
A forever-date into light & dark places.

Hard to shake
It is a jigsaw puzzle.
Layered & complex
Quiet yet requires a muzzle.

Once You figure trauma out
It will check out.
Or Checkmate
When grieving Kings and Queens debate.

Trauma feeds on fear
So don't let it permeate.
Don't invite it to dinner
Entertaining…makes it easy to congregate.

Trauma knows your bail bond
Persistently it will reach out.
Do not negotiate with terrorists
Call for help, do the hard work and pray until you get out.

written by Charmaine 'C-Maine' Jennings

YOU ARE VICTORIOUS

SPILL THE SWEET TEA & LEMONADE!!!

What has trauma taught you? How did it impact you and your marriage?

HIS TRUTH

Trauma, like so many other words in our English vernacular, can be a very subjective term. In many ways, what we typically see are the "effects" of trauma and those things are often used to guide us back to the experience or source.

One of the things that I learned about trauma is that not everyone is impacted by the same things or in the same ways. What may have been a part of your cultural norm that you attribute to strength and resilience, may serve as a catastrophic moment in the lifepath of someone else. This is one of the primary reasons why so many people become intensely guarded about their challenges. It can serve as an offshoot of the "Oppression Olympics," where comparison with other people minimizes the impact of our experiences. If we're not careful, we will find ourselves mired in embarrassment and shame because of the mental isolation.

This is why we must remain committed to understanding our WHO and WHY: Who am I as a person? Why am I the way that I am? What factors and circumstances contributed to my condition? These questions are uncomfortable, but also necessary in helping to target trauma points and identify the work required to be healthy and whole. No one could do that for me. It was an individual decision that I had to keep for myself.

I was fortunate. As I genuinely pursued the answers to my struggles, I was guided toward individuals and organizations that held me accountable. My life connected me with people and opportunities that coincide with my path. However, how many of those things did I overlook because I was trying to run from myself? How much time did I spend denying how my past was affecting my present? It reminds me of a quote from one of my favorite books, The Alchemist: "To realize one's Personal Legend is a person's only real obligation... and, when you want something, all the universe conspires in helping you to achieve it." The trauma that transpired in my life wasn't seamless, but I do believe that it worked and is working for my good (Romans 8:28) in both my individual life and marriage.

HER TRUTH

Couples should be open to courageous conversations about acute, chronic, and complex trauma. When Walter and I were dating and married, we both shared several personal stories that included: crisis, betrayals, disappointments, and hardships. Although these discussions fostered trust, transparency, and vulnerability... we still didn't have the skills to go deeper in-order-to understand the impact. We needed skills and strategies to process how the residue of our trauma was showing up in our relationships. We both thought that we were healthy, but that wasn't the reality. Now what?

Trauma taught me that bad things happen to good people and good things happen to bad people. Maybe life wasn't going to be fair, but it was definitely going to show up every day and do its job. My concentration needed to be...Am I committed to doing my job? I needed to focus on what I was going to do to make my life experiences count. How could I heal, overcome, and conquer the heartbreaks? Trauma taught me that I was resilient and persistent (i.e. good-stubborn). It taught me that my 5 names were a force to be reckoned with and that God was very intentional. He knew that he could count on me to use my voice and experiences to help other people.

I entered our marriage with high levels of complex trauma. I was not conscious of how my adverse childhood experiences (i.e., ACE score) shaped my wants, needs, and desires to feel safe in a relationship. The first seven years of my life were spent in foster care. I experienced loss, grief, abandonment, and sexual abuse to name a few. As a result, I was insecure and lacked a sense of safety and protection by others. I learned that at the first sign of people not claiming me or believing me...that I needed to protect myself. This eventually led me to stop waiting for people to show up overall. I learned that I had to be the leader in my own rescue story. Of course...this was not a fully balanced recipe for trusting my life partner or to recover when problems surfaced. Thank God for my parents who gave me the best gift ever. They introduced me to the Lord and modeled the power of love, family, and forgiveness.

SLAVE-STYLE

You talk about someone with problems:
My life is more troublesome
than random sex with no condom.

Issues keep pressing me,
so writing has become my therapy.

By no means have I cut the lines of communication,
but the things that I'm facing
keep my mental impatient.

I've been sleeping a lot lately,
no I don't have a baby
it's just that in order to escape the heat
or face defeat
I choose to go on mental retreats.

When I'm awake
I dodge and fake,
hiding behind bottles and tobacco
substances unnatural
but my nerves are shot to hell
or can't you tell?

Look into my eyes as I pass you,
I know you wonder what I've been through,
    and perhaps I should mention the suicidal tendencies that plague
                                                                    me.

I'm a slave to my thoughts
and my Black and Mild box,
perhaps I'm captive to the vodka I just bought,
when I get a break from my masters
I record my disasters,
hoping it's something I can look back on
and see where I've come from,
praying I'm not making predictions
would rather be healing inflictions
as you can see I have several.

We slaves get whipped pretty rough,
but when I've had enough
I look my master in his eyes and say
"Hey!
If that whip cracks my back again
I'll get to snapping arms and limbs,
make your eyes swell up until your vision gets dim.
Now as I flee this plantation you better not chase,
I worked hard for too long,
now let me leave this place."

written by Walter 'Wally-B' Jennings

BREAK DOWN

Break Down 1
Break Down 2
Break Down 3
Break Down 4

What happens when your life
is exiting the building?
When death is knocking at the door?

Mid Life,
Before life,
After Life,
Husband & Wife,
Girlfriend,
Boyfriend,
Best Friends,
Policeman,
Simply…Human.

Break-ups and Breakdowns
happen all of the time.
Especially when the left and right brain
are not fully aligned.

Chemically imbalanced
Closed for repairs.
Logic and Reasoning
in despair.

Deaf, Creative
and a blind heart.
A recipe for building
an upside down Noah's Ark.

It does NOT work
Only drowns and hurts
all parties involved.

A mystery unsolved
because there are too many players.
Too many lanes
and too many layers.

Racing for the number one spot.
Crashing into the side rail
thinking is this the finale,
climax, or surprise plot?

Where is the emergency siren?
Where is your very talented pit crew?
The people that you trust
with big passion are only a select few.

Those who normally can build-up
what has just broken down?
For 10 minutes you wait and reflect
but no one is around.

Your mind plays tug-of-war,
Saying you're wrong
But also right.
You've lost,

but stand your ground,
Suck it up, don't lose this fight.

This is your fault,
Or is it mine?
Fixing the problem
Without collaboration isn't fine.

Now Doubt, Fear,
and Insecurity
Divide you
by controlling the situation.

The Jaws of Life Can't save you
Thick metals and plastic have you trapped.
Your transmission died and
Yesterday the car insurance lapsed.

You are Charlie Brown
Or coal miners trapped inside a 60-foot hole.
Bad luck lingers on you
like cheap cologne.

Rhetorical,
the check engine light flashes on
Gasping for water
to cool its throat in song.

It's the ultimate breakup-breakdown
In the street, or on the curb
On the expressway, across-town or midtown
Any location will serve.

On the shoulder or in the median,
Downtown or on the boulevard
On the highway or interstate
You never expected it to be this hard.

The brake pads didn't work
The gas pedal is pressed down.
Rural, urban, Suburban
No matter which part of town.

It's broken and you can't fix it
What's worse is you can't lift it.
The burdens and the smoke are all coming from your chest.
They get heavier with every single breath.

Your head is like the engine,
lately, always running hot.
Your heart is pumping fast,
Stuck and unable to leave this spot.

The seat belt is a snake squeezing and choking you.
Although it also keeps you alive.
The door is jammed,
but you are trying to survive.

Other cars speed by
You hope that someone sees you.
Your life is in neutral
But signaling for help is impossible to do.

Your strongest personality trait
and biggest upsetting weakness.
Pride comes before the fall

Emotions bleed like shameful secrets.

No surprise, the nearest exit is 100 miles
An hour until sundown and 12 more til sunrise.
This breakdown seems like your conclusion,
An Australian rock-bottom down under illusion.

Things are currently rough
But is this your time to shine?
Are you missing an opportunity,
Because the next rest stop is another 5 miles?

You may be the light
For someone else's rest.
Do not fail to live
By choosing to protest.

While others gain a roadside peace prize
Resilient, they build up.
If you break down
Scream for help and don't let up.

Check-in with a friend
Or a mental health professional.
Unplug
Tame the toxic voices and conflicting sounds.
Your village is ready to work
If you invite them to come around.
If they ask you where you are and what do you need?
Just respond....

Mid Life,
Before life

After Life,
Husband & Wife.
Girlfriend,
Boyfriend
Best Friends,
Policeman or simply,
A Human Experience.

Break-ups and Breakdowns
happen all of the time.
Especially when the left and right brain
are not aligned.

Chemically imbalanced,
Closed for repairs.
A mystery unsolved
because there are too many players
To many lanes
and too many layers.

Racing
for the number one spot.
Crashing into the side rail.
thinking is this your finale, climax, or plot?

Where is the emergency siren?
Where is your very talented pit crew?
The people that you trust
with big passion are only a select few.

Those who normally can
Build up
what has just broken down

For 10 minutes you wait and reflect,
but no one is around
Only your thoughts,
Actions,
and God.

written by Charmaine 'C-Maine' Jennings

SELF-ANALYSIS

We all have faults.
We all have...
imperfections
and spiritual infections
that we attempt to keep concealed,
we keep it locked and sealed,
then in the same breath
holla to..."keep it real."
Because in reality,
we all want to appear as if we've got it together,
we've
got it better
than what we know is inside,
and with no ends tied
we find ourselves drifting further and further from the truth,
faces with no identity,
like John Doe in the news,
we are
merely
playing a part,
desecrating an art
because the world's most influential expressions
originate in the heart.

We all have faults.
We all have...
checkered pasts
and a bone path
that lead to that party in our closet.
...that closet

that artists
go to for inspiration,
for motivation on their next move,
because your skeletons chase you,
they race you
to see exactly how far you will go
so that no one will know
what is in your closet,
what broken promises
& lies
comprise
their existence.

I have faults.
I have...
imperfections
and spiritual infections
that I try to keep concealed,
yet and still
I find myself exposing my secrets,
because I know if I keep it
I will only be compounding embarrassment with guilt,
spiritually killed
because I'm internally
burning,
yearning to be free from what I know,
so I....
let it go.

I have faults.
I have...
a checkered past
and a bone path

that lead to my closet,
but as an artist...
as a man that has spent
so much time lying
trying
to hide things,
I'm slowly finding
that there is freedom
by admitting,
I have issues.

I have issues,
and miscues
that exist beyond your mind's comprehension,
and in no way am I in any position
to look down or judge anyone,
no matter what walk of life you come from
I feel that there is always something to learn from everyone.
But...
some of us have become excellent liars,
excellent hiders
of our own transgressions,
so when life's lessons
are taught by someone we perceive as inferior,
we ain't even hearin ya!
...and many of us are so philosophical
that it has become impossible
for anyone else to get in a word,
so busy giving advice
we forget that sometimes,
hurting people just want to be heard.
I make sure to keep my heart & mind open,
hoping

to capture new lessons taught to me,
because I'm incomplete.
I have faults
and talks
with myself to remind me
that my poetry
is a chance for me to make things right,
to affect someone else's life,
so that they will not crash in the same hole
on the same road
that I once traveled.

…and as I fight with low self-esteem,
alcoholism,
& depression,
it's a blessing
that I'm even able to stand before you today,
and it's the reason why I stay
and listen to all those that wish to converse and build,
because the world is filled
with people that are so busy analyzing someone else,
that we don't take time to check ourselves.
We don't take time to see
what we used to be.
…and if we really
I mean
REALLY
appreciated how far we've come,
we'd yield the floor to those in despair
and not be so quick to judge.

written by Walter 'Wally-B' Jennings

LETTERS OF THE LOST

Riddle me this?
What is the most important letter in a stream of 26?

It is definitely a vowel,
Not a random sound.
It is necessary to accomplish the goal of "Valedictorian,"
For which it has appeared twice.

It might tell you...

It has the right to remain silent
To take lavish public beach trips.
It wears skinny diphthongs
Like beautiful people who sit and sip.

It is an obvious treasure
For those seeking to find gold
Not a confused rainbow
Or a closeted kinky fantasy on hold.

This letter has a true identity,
It does not need to self-announce, redefine, or uncover.
It does not manipulate,
Lie or cause others to suffer.

It does not need to trick or convince.

It is "A" accountable
It seeks to "H" help and heal.

Not by "F" force, but by "C" choice
It gives "L" love, it does not "S" steal.

It is Nonbinary,
A loyal member of the 26-letter family.

At family reunions, it is always first,
It never arrives last.
It supports the child who wanders aimlessly
Transformed into a social outcast.

It is ready when a little girl's bedroom trauma arrives,
Before she masters her multiplication facts.
Before she learns suffixes and prefixes?
When virginity is uncertain although her hymen is intact?

This letter listens to a child
When marked, recruited, and preyed on years later as a tween.
Questioning who would believe her
When she doesn't belong to anyone or have anything.

So what is the story?
Pace yourself.
Can you handle the truth?
Listen and brace yourself.

Two young girls regularly
played with dolls behind closed doors.
A little brother is in the room,
but told to close his eyes and sit on the floor.

But, At whose expense?

My "I" innocence left,
and bad intentions came.
With "F" fear her 7yr old brother complied,
So at the age of 5, I did the same

"T" touched and "V" violated
For her sexual pleasures and desires.
Afterwards, I was alone and scared
I was left to answer and inquire.

Do I like girls?
Am I different or "G" gay now?
Sitting in the shame of... "after."
Playing with dolls could never be the same, how?

At the age of 5, I didn't know the word sex,
Nor this type of weird alphabet
"V" for victim, "A" for abuse, "P" for predator or prey
What did it actually mean to be "G" gay?

"C" confused about everything.
"A" ashamed because I was unable to say, N.O. "no."
"B" but could I?
When I was the "F" foster child living in her grandparents' home.

I was just a guest.
Easily invited and easily sent away
"Nothing to no one."
Is what I learned to say,

Who would repair a tongue out-of-order
I was Valedictorian of the graduating class of Poverty
I wasn't strong enough to wage war

She had the ultimate authority.

Her privilege tall and heavy like a giant,
I weighed into this fight…too little
Water against blood
A public defender against a judge
Thunder versus lightning
Puma against Nike
Who would be in my corner to support me?

She was the most important letter in her family's alphabet
The "A" apple to their eye while I was just a reject.
Her personal sexual tool to be explored and used
But who taught her these pedophilia rules?

She was probably being abused too
A muse for some disgusting adult's foreplay.
A small letter in their fresh soup of the day
She wasn't born this way!!!

Gender fluid, expressing
Identifying & exploring,
These distracting questions were homework.
Emotionally storming and intellectually pouring.

The LGBTQ world I wasn't born into
I just wanted a real friend
I wanted an "A" ally
An A+ friend.

Instead she delivered an alphabet of confusion
Not the most important letter in a stream of 26
Not a random sound

Not the first vowel but a stream of consonants

Not an accomplished Valedictorian
For which this important letter appears twice
I lost my innocent expectation
For other children to play nice

Once I was forced to remain silent
but not as an educator of today
No more hidden consonants
Letters gain power by what they say

No longer seeking to find friendship gold
Especially if it's handcuffed by a rainbow
I can discern those who flex the rules.
Those seeking to use deceptive excavation tools.

Those roaming the streets and blocks
Those who alter a child's novice-level spelling.
Those who recruit them before they can read
or process what the adult (i.e. the sexually mature) is even selling.

Let's keep their combination of letters away
Stop the toxic yet hidden agendas.
Children should be free to be children
Not exploited by predatory lenders.

Let's become an "A" ally and advocate
Let's be watchmen standing at innocence's gate
Let sing the original alphabet song
Without exchanging early memories of purity… with hate

Let's keep bedroom doors open

To remain vigilant and see.
Let's inspect what we expect
Let's know what's happening.

It only takes one bad letter
to ruin an entire word
It infects the heart and numbs the tongue
It can paralyze every verb.

May this letter never be lost
The cost was too high.
May we rewrite the song of the innocent,
May responsibility not die.

May this letter affirm healing harmony
By the melodic sound of survivors
Those whose inner child desperately longs
To recite the ABCs in private,
Public
And without prejudice.

written by Charmaine 'C-Maine' Jennings

⌘

CHAPTER SIX
"Children Ain't Kids"
Parenting Privileges

HOT QUESTION #1: What is the best part about becoming a parent? What is the most challenging part of parenting? Explain.

Charmaine

The best part about becoming a parent was seeing my infant daughters sleep in perfect peace. I love seeing them happy and succeeding in their areas of interest like performing or creating. I also enjoy that they represent bits and pieces of Walter and I. The most challenging part about parenting is that our daughters represent bits and pieces of Walter and me. God is amazing. He has an exceptional sense of humor. I believe that He puts a mirror in your face to help you grow and develop. Typically, your children are that mirror. Children are God's way of saying if you want to know if you need to mature in the areas of love, joy, peace, patience, kindness, goodness, faithfulness, gentleness, and self-control... then sign up to become a parent.

Walter

The best part of parenting has been the opportunity to see portions of yourself and your spouse show up in these "little people." It is literally a science experiment where you see what happens when you combine two people into one person. Some of my favorite moments were watching our daughters do something and turning to Charmaine and saying, "That's you, right there!" Ironically, this is also the most challenging part of parenting. You don't get to pick which attributes your children will possess. How do you discipline your children when they display less-than-desirable traits that came directly from you? Also, what happens when they begin growing into their own unique personality that is foreign to you?

HOT QUESTION #2: Is it more difficult to parent an under-age child or an adult child? Explain.

Charmaine

I believe that it is more difficult to parent adult children. Fortunately, adult children have seen your positive behaviors and strengths, but unfortunately, they have also seen your inconsistencies and flaws. This can provide learning opportunities for both of you to grow, talk, and bond. However, if judgment, contention, and disdain develop it could negatively change the relationship dynamic that results in a lack of respect. Adult children have their own autonomy and manage their own circle of control. I realized that I only have influence, not control after a certain time. I am committed to utilizing my parental power to make a difference. This means that I chose to listen more than I speak and offer advice and wisdom when requested. It may require watching as my children stumble. I trust that they will find value in wisdom and pursue it. This is the hard part, which makes parenting adult children more difficult, but not impossible.

Walter

It's not even close. It is definitely more difficult parenting adult children. You tend to have a lot more latitude and influence with under-age children. They are typically more dependent and apt to come to you for help. This often allows you to be proactive before situations become dire. Adult children utilize their independence to take more risks...often to their detriment! In a lot of ways, it's like watching your child learn how to walk again. However, the consequences of them falling are significantly more damaging. I will say that it can be very rewarding to arrive at a place of newfound respect with your adult children. It is a blessing when their life experiences humble them in such a way that they appreciate you not only as their parents, but as fellow adults.

THE DECLARATION OF DEPENDANTS

We,
the couple of Walter & Charmaine
maintain
& hold these truths to be self-evident
that we are young, married, and childless.

Contrary to popular belief
or the word on the street
There's absolutely nothing wrong with us.

Rumors of our physical shortcomings
are just thoughtless rumblings
from individuals eager to make us parents,
so allow me to make this apparent:
My sperm count is fine
and she has fully functional eggs
so please rest your head
and stop asking yourself:
"Why don't they have children?"

Better still
allow me if you will
to pose these questions:
Why are we on your timetable?
We chose to refrain
beyond your timeframe
and now we're unable?
Something has to be wrong?

She and I get along
and we've been married a year and a half
I mean,
people are actually mad!
Upset to the point that they flat-out embarrass themselves,
questioning us about our sex life
and I'm like...what the hell?!
We both know that there's no such thing as an ideal situation to
have a child,
but that doesn't mean we're going to go buck wild
and have children because we can,
because she's my wife and I'm her man,
Please understand that we both take this very seriously.

It would be foolish of us to rush into parenthood without thinking
things through,
love does conquer all...but we use our brains too!
The same brains that got us college certificates,
which is one of the reasons why our parents are livid
because they feel as though we should be making no less than 40
Grand,
but I'm even more confused,
because if our families fused
you could count about 40 Grands,
I don't understand the big hurry
or the flurry of questions
about what we're waiting for,
as much as they complain about loans
are you sure you want more?

I found the whole situation hilarious,
people think they're scaring us

or applying pressure,
but Charmaine and I are in this together,
and any decision we make is because we wanted to,
so if we wanted two or three
that's exactly how it will be,
but we pay you people no mind
and take our time
because y'all don't see the bottom line.

We might be young and energetic,
but we're also stubborn and hard-headed
with a fetish for dancing and seafood,
a candlelit sea cruise
and as this romance continues
you need not concern yourselves about when our babies will drop,
because after the fourth you will have a new question like
"Man, when are they going to stop!?"

written by Walter 'Wally-B' Jennings

A BEAUTIFUL SURPRISE

Simone is beautiful, no surprise
A teacher in a hard category.
She sees minor things
Like conformations of prophecy.

Eyeglass lens because I can't see
She is a modern-day prodigy.
Who speaks without sound
She pierces hearts deep down.

She is loud, yet silent
Tall...yet small.
Blinks eyes & flaps hands
When many people are involved.

She is valuable
A gift you'll never forget.
The largest amount of money You've ever spent.

She teaches lesson one
Get rid of your big fat ego.
Take random barefoot walks
Feel the earth between your toes.

Do not look around
To see who's watching.
Once a week swing on a swing
Imagination will kidnap reality.

Run into a huge closet

Play hide-and-seek.
Turn the lights off
So eyes do not deceive.

Any second now
You might be found.
Wait for it...
Wait for it...

By the giggling crescendo
Simone seeks & peeks.
Ready to be seen and
Tickled uncontrollably.

She preaches lesson two
Blowing bubbles actually sooth.
They float for a few seconds
Leaving a lasting impression.

Their color does not matter!
They remain light and free.
Their color does not matter!
They land wherever they please.

She illuminates the soul
Her complexion is iridescent.
She dances in the sun
Her love is effervescent.

Simone can deter race wars Before they have begun.
She refuses to kill the harmony Of innocent fun.

Please read her dissertation

Her argument clearly states,
I know why the world is a mess
It is obvious why people hate.

Adopt iridescent states-of-mind
Our similarities make us kind.
What makes us different makes us "one"
Positive words & actions eliminate guns.

Victory…
Is at the playground.
Bottle empty
Bubbles flying around.

Are adults happy and sound?
Are adults confident and free?
Do they realize
They too…have special needs?

Battling a spectrum of sensory,
Vocal chords handcuffed-yet fighting.
Social skills have stubborn will,
Zero medications or pharmaceutical pills.

She embodies lesson three
Obsessed with jump therapy
When was the last time you soared?
Remove both feet up off the floor.

When bent knees fly free
Bounce like a vibrant baby.
Drink from the fountain of youth
Once you weren't afraid to.

Eat what you want!
Pancakes for dinner.
Pizza or salad for breakfast
Calories are returned to the sender.

Wear soothing clothes
Non-itchy textiles or doilies.
No need to mix and match
If you're colorblind?
No worries.

Simone displays bold confidence,
Filled with zero apologies.
A leader of social groups,
Her resilience is bulletproof.

Simone is inspiration
A reason to smile.
She set others free
She is an inclusive profile

Simone means 'God has heard.'
Jaslyn, God's fragrant flower & protected.
Talese means God's consecrated, Lovely water and peace.
God is gracious, equals Jennings because He sees.

She is my daughter
An expression of God's love
A one-of-a-kind gift
A single white dove.

She is a truth

That tells no lies.
A master teacher
My beautiful iridescent surprise.

written by Charmaine 'C-Maine' Jennings

GOD GAVE ME GIRLS

…and so he told me
…upon hearing the news
that I'm about to have daughter #2
that "real men make men,
and since I can't seem to pass on
my Y chromosome
then I must not have what it takes to train one
let alone make one,"
he says all of this while watching me tutor his son.
Algebra.
…combining "like terms."
Learn
the value of x and y
by isolating the variable to one side
and I…
can't lie,
secretly it does hurt,
because a man's worth
can often be tied to his ability to procreate males
regardless of whether or not he stays,
and every man dreams of having a son someday,
someone to carry on his last name,
and somehow make up for all the mistakes he made,
but…GOD gave me girls,
and since I believe in destiny,
and not fate,
I have to trust that GOD planned it this way,
I'm just not sure why,
maybe He wanted me to see what it was like to be on the opposite
side

of the games I used to play,
I mean,
I used to hear it a lot,
but when did you ever think about a girl's father before you took her
out?
What it must have been like to be in his shoes
and the fact that you
could be him one day,
or maybe because of the way
the world is headed
He knew I'd teach my daughters to be warrior women,
or maybe…He just wanted me to be thankful for what I was given,
because how many times have you gotten exactly what you asked for
and regretted that you asked for it?
How many times were you absolutely certain
that if you got the person
you wanted you'd be happy,
only to realize that there's a reason you keep picking men that remind
you of your daddy?
or women that remind you of your mother
and the qualities you would've like to see in them?
…in him,
in her,
the first
relationship we ever forge with the opposite sex,
is with our parents,
regardless of whether they're present or absent
and since
GOD gave me girls,
I'm charged with setting a good example,
handling my business
regardless of what the situation is,
THAT'S what real men do…

I aced Algebra II
because I always knew
how to find the value of X and Y,
isolate boys and girls to opposite sides
and you'll find
that although their needs are different,
their values are equivalent,
congruent
when it comes to a father's influence,
and I use my patience
to keep the equation
balanced,
and if you think it takes more talent
to train your son:
Talk to me when your child runs up to you asking
if they're matching
because they were dressed by their mother,
and when it comes to fashion
they don't really trust her,
not like they trust their daddy,
get at me
when you spend your Friday evenings
greasing
your child's hair with a jar of Sulfur 8
and spend 2 hours trying to get "the line" in the middle of their hair
straight,
holla at me
when you have to take your child to the bathroom in public
but they can't touch nothing…
so you have to hold them up over the toilet seat
and pray to GOD you don't get hit with pee,
tell me

you know the theme song to Hannah Montana, Dora the Explorer, or
High School Musical
and then maybe you can relate to what I'm going through,
until then
I'll be waiting for your son
on the front lawn
with a shotgun,
a bathrobe,
church socks,
and house slippers,
just so he remembers
that when he takes out Charmione or Simone,
they're never really alone
so bring them back home
the same way that they left,
because when GOD gives girls,
He gives us...the best.

written by Walter 'Wally-B' Jennings

DAUGHTER DIARIES

What do I tell a mother
At a Christian Women's conference?
She aggressively asked me
How should she have responded?

Her daughter told her she is a lesbian.
She said, "Lately my life hasn't felt like Heaven."

"My heart is an unanswered letter, so preach…preacher!
Speak…speaker!
What more do you have to say?
I pray every day…but my daughter's 'gay' ain't going away."

Her eye gaze…. highlighted her grief.
Defeated…she "slow-motion" sat down in her seat.
Desperate to find answers and cures for her daughter's sexual preferences
I knew that if I offered options yet solid suggestions,
It would still offend and send her deeper into her depression.

So… All I could say was Matthew 6:33
"Seek ye first the kingdom of God and its righteousness. And all these things will be added unto you."
Proverbs 3:5-6 "Trust in the Lord with all of your heart, lean not unto your own understanding, acknowledge Him and He will direct your path."

Perhaps this mother,
Desired Psalms 23:4
A rod and staff to comfort her daughter

All the days of her life

Maybe she would dwell
In the house of the Lord forever.

I asked her,
"Is it possible that your daughter
Doesn't want a relationship with Christ?
Because she has never
Met or seen a real Christian?

Is it possible that she is spiritually anemic?
Is she thirsting for real love and truth?
Because she isn't getting it from you?

Mother
When was the last time you said, "I love you?"
With no strings attached.
Giving her attention and hugs
Always having her back.

Your daughter is saying,
"I hope that you can learn to love me
Currently. At this very moment!
Regardless of my sexuality
Even though our relationship forecast is partly cloudy."

"Is your God big enough?
To shine His son's light?
On ME, on WE and on US?
Can we respectfully agree?
And disagree in love?"

After seeing the intensity in this mother's eyes,

I knew that she was about to cry.
Her fight was not with me
but with grief.

The death of a dream.
Will her daughter give her grandchildren
After marrying the nice boy next door?
Her plan was crumbling before her eyes
Her daughter's announcement caught her by surprise.

Perhaps my answer was a partial translation of her daughter's words,
All of which she'd already heard.

In all of our getting we are to get full understanding.
Are we having a conversation about identity or sexuality?
Identity is about purpose
Sexuality is about preferred practices.

Mother...
The next time your daughter asks you to watch a 30 second trailer
Of her motion picture "life story."
Just give God the glory
Listen in love.
Share her identity through God's lens,
Do not be distracted.

Her sexuality is between her and Him.
Her life experiences and free-will decisions
Are not controlled by you.
Pray and fast and He will tell you exactly what to do.

Knowledge is knowing the right answers,
Intelligence is asking the right questions.
Wisdom is using your heart and ears

To guide your actions.

So from one mother to another...
In all of your getting, get understanding
Lead and GUIDE her by listening and asking
Cast your role as an advocate and support.
God's plan and process does not always align with yours.

Allow her to meet and see a real Christian
No matter if the discussion gets heated,
No matter if both your personalities get fiery,
Be thankful
She is putting a voice
To the most intimate page
Of her secret diary.

I know this emotional work is HARD!
You may not want to do the work
But You...were chosen, for this challenge, for such a time as this

That's Why...
Heavily guarded with a lock and key
These are the things typically never said...
To a fragile mother
Out loud!

written by Charmaine 'C-Maine' Jennings

⌘

CHAPTER SEVEN
Relation...Slips: Ignorance Is Bliss or Causes Blisters

Relationships are a cornerstone of happiness and living a full life. A healthy relationship is priceless because it helps to reduce stress, increase healing potential, promotes positive behaviors, and provides a sense of purpose which helps couples live longer. The bliss of a happy relationship flourishes when couples communicate and invest in lifelong dating. A balance of playing, working, and living fosters synergy and strong levels of physical, spiritual, and emotional intimacy.

Relation...Slips represent the mistakes, betrayals, and harmful behaviors that occur with friends, community, work colleagues, and romantic partners. If you slip and fall on a wet floor, it is difficult to get up on your own. Support is helpful and you may need to get up slowly and approach your next steps with care and thoughtful consideration. Although no one typically plans to have a relation...slip, we should be slow to judge, seek first to understand, and learn to forgive.

Couples who learn from their mistakes make history. Their story includes resilience, stamina, grace, mercy, and compassion. These skills gathered through "yearning-learning" moments are highly valuable. They can provide a level of understanding only found through experience. It is easier for couples to walk away but harder to stay and clean the mess up. "Ignorance is Bliss" is a dangerous and misleading mentality. Not knowing is not a gift to the relationship. There is no peace in hoarding the truth or being deceived by the person you love. The lack of transparency means that trust is non-existent. A relationship without trust is love anemic and feels more like a transaction. Love hard because love is hard.

LOVE'S INSPIRATION

It's a second look,

but sometimes,

it's a LOOOOOONG first look.

It's an introduction.

It's an exchange of phone numbers.

It's waiting on him to call.

It's him waiting to call so he doesn't look too anxious.

It's a conversation.

She laughs.

It's a conversation.

He nods.

It's a conversation.

Communication.

It's natural.

It's the best part of your day.

It's...feeling strange when you don't speak.

It's talking so much you miss sleep.

...miss shows.

...miss your homegirls.

...miss games.

It's people seeing the change before you do.

It's wanting to be seen WITH you

it's, NOT "Netflix and Chill"

it's, let's go on a date FOR REAL!

It's going to see a movie she picked but complained about.

It's going to see a movie he picked but fell asleep on.

It's spending $100 to win her a $25 teddy bear at the fair.

It's trying to impress her.

It's her acting like she's not.

It's trying to impress him

and getting mad when he acts like he's not.

It's argue

breakup
makeup.

It's argue
breakup
makeup.

It's argue
breakup
hold up…

It's standing at a crossroad.

It's deciding if we're moving on together or alone.

It's recognizing I'm better with you than without you.

So instead of argue

breakup

makeup.

It's just argue

make up.

It's… times getting tough and we stand strong.

It's… phone calls for no reason.

It's text messages for no reason.

It's…flowers for no reason.

It's not letting go of your hand through every season.

It's being thankful for all the wrong ones that help you appreciate the right one.

It's you like it and you want it…then put a ring on it!

It's you get me…you get my WHOLE family!

It's for better or worse.

It's…our worth isn't based on where we work.

It's for richer or poorer.

It's…first houses and foreclosures.

It's visiting the doctor…but no weapon formed against us shall prosper.

It's till death do us part.

It's the start of forever.

It's L.O.V.E.:

Living Out Volatile Expressions.

Learning Our Values Everyday.

Looking Over Vanity's Efforts.

No matter how much weight we gain

No matter how our hair may change

It's "Same Ol' Love" by Anita Baker

It's not always getting it right

...but still bring your behind home every night!

It's...you don't deserve it...but I forgive you!

It's...I didn't deserve it...but He forgave me!

We are a 3-strand cord not easily broken

It's being angry...

...frustrated

but still knowing

no relationship will ever work

until I commit to loving Christ and myself first

It's Love's Inspiration.

Always believing

Never failing

because in the never-ending fight for our lives

Love.

…with its head humbly bowed and our hearts still beating in its
battle-worn hands
it will always be the last one standing.

Perfect.

Undefeated.

Inspiring us…to do the same.

written by Walter 'Wally-B' Jennings

JUST WANT TO LOVE YOU

"I wanna love you
And treat you right
I want to love you,
Every day and every night
We'll be together
With a roof up over your head
We'll share the shelter of our single bed"
Is this Love, Is the Love, Is this Love, Is this Love that I'm feeling."
~Bob Marley

What happens when my heart stops beating
for what your heart and body bleed for?
Yet you stand at the door and knock
But I'm not ready, or dressed… so I completely ignore.

I say, "Just leave me and don't come back!
Don't worry, it's not your fault, It's me and not you!"
I am not ready for a real relationship
You're so serious, and I am still going through.

But you reply and…say
you're not finished with me yet
You see me!
Still failing every test.

Breaking promises
with tear-stained tissues
You already know
that I have really big issues.

But you keep coming here
and I don't know why.
It's like your motives are actually pure
or You need a credible alibi.

You say, "You want to be my one and true passion...
You keep telling me that you are my man."
You want me to hear your powerful voice
Beyond space and time you truly understand?

Me. You say that I am made perfect
I am so very worth it,
This is why you stand at the door and knock
That's why you are here?!

You don't care about my Earthly flaws
That's why you are here?!
You know that I can't conquer them alone,
THAT'S! WHY! YOU ARE HERE!

That's why I shouldn't try
to figure this out on my own?
Billions of people before me
got it wrong.

They attempted
by exercising their own stubborn will
Tried but left the earth
with cold lifeless bodies made stiff and still.

But not you...you are real

Your soothing words

are a gift that is heartfelt
The best type of help.

A precious lamb,
My daily bread
The only way to keep me
out of my analytical head.

Away from logic and reasoning
the harshness of the law.
To restore the earth
and its rigid tasteless seasoning,
with the salt that You created in me.

To bring back love into this community
and feed the hunger in the streets.
where the Gentiles live
and beg for real meat.

You don't need a pretty building
or want a graven image.
Just my heart and adoration
without any limits.

You want to teach me how to Love
Because Love is Your Name
Love is who you are
Not a noun, verb, or bank account of unhealthy scars.

You just want to love me
You are the bridegroom and I am the bride.
You just want to love me
I am your best possession and prize.

I am your most precious creation and sacrifice
You died once, but lived twice.
You saved the best for last
To secure my future, while forgetting my past.

I don't owe you anything
You have no expectations.
You just want to love me
and I have to grow up.
and learn just how
to receive
an authentic Love like this.

written by Charmaine 'C-Maine' Jennings

CHEATERS NEVER WIN 2.0

King Kong ain't got nothing on me!!!
Lifetime movies make satire of Marvel & DC.
Shakespeare classics become junk mail
When you play the cheat game…you automatically fail.

Cheaters never win
They steal, grin, and spin.
They are more dangerous than the CIA
So entitled…they never want to pay.

Cheaters work hard to draw a line in the sand
Dare you to be confident…while they take your man.
Strategically studying all of your weaknesses
They gather intel about your past & present secrets.

They test relationship fragility by casting their bait
Pretend to respect marriage when their loyalty is fake.
They are the best empathetic ears…for your relationship problems
They flirt, twerk, and speak about 300 ways to solve them.

They wrap a 20% lie, in the 80% truth
Wear innocent clothing to manipulate and seduce.
They cling to the wealth of men who are taken
They hurt because they're hurt and flirt with temptation.

They become available and saleable
Merchandise that's marketable and profitable.
But at what price will they enjoy being cheap?
Passionate nights equal conception in back seats.

With or without shame
The husband returns back home.
Wifey pretends to be sleeping
In their bed alone.

But she is consumed with doubt and wonder
Intrusive thoughts flood mental moments with toxic clutter.
Adamant that absence was because he is well-employed
The working late expectation wasn't supposed to return void.

Her gynecologist
Proved this theory to be a lie.
A positive STD test
Demoted her from "wife" to "ride or die."

She gave him 6 babies,
a shared house, money, cars, life insurance, and IRAs.
She is close to his boss
Could get him fired any day.

So he creeps into bed to go to sleep
Uncomfortable, sleeps with one eye open and peeps.
He is "sin-sick" and trust is hazy
He arrogantly cheated and blamed her for being crazy.

Gaslighting and deflecting boomeranged
Shots were fired and he was hit.
He hasn't seen crazy yet
He struck the match and now…wifey's pissed.

Her plan was easy
Be committed and queen-befitted.

Focus on wealth and health
Assess if he is "affair-fantasy" addicted.

She caters an expensive dinner
Put "biochemical organisms" in his fancy green beans.
Diarrhea promoted the toilet, "best friend"
It took weeks to heal his "disease of mean."

Wifey hired a private investigator
Uncovered where the "affair partner" lives and works.
Identified her contacts, associates, and friends
She hit her where it hurts.

Submitted 100 anonymous customer complaints
Made her miserable until she quit.
Accessed her social security number
Destroyed her perfect credit.

Wifey was crazy about reclaiming her life
Their cheating caused this pain & strife.
Love and loyalty provoked her wrath
Winning means protecting her marriage.

Till death does her marriage part
The war of Infidelity left a horrific mark.
It's lose-lose because cheaters never win
But neither do the scorned or recipients of revenge.

written by Charmaine 'C-Maine' Jennings

⌘

CHAPTER EIGHT
Tap Dancing On
My Haiku Nerves:
Are We Gon Make It?!

Relationships help to reveal if each of us is guilty of exhibiting signs of being passive, petty, or nurturing a pet peeve. Passive means not actively responding or resisting by accepting or allowing what is happening or being done. Petty means that you care too much about small or minor things of importance. This also means a person who behaves in a mean, unkind or tit-for-tat manner. For example, if you date your friend's ex because they betrayed you and dated your ex. A pet peeve is something that you find extremely yet frequently annoying. For example, when people misinterpret words or when they misuse your words. Millions of couples and non-romantic relationships engage in conflict. Our response is typically on trial and listed as one of these three, so let's test the theory.

A PET PEEVE, PETTY, OR PASSIVE?

Read the statements below and decide if the situation or response is petty, passive, or a pet peeve.

1. The silent treatment.
2. Not responding to text messages or missed calls.
3. When a person says, "I'm fine" but their actions/tone says, "I'm not fine."
4. Comparing your partner to other people.
5. Changing your behavior around friends or family.
6. Refusing to apologize or refusing to ask for help.
7. Saying, "I told you so…" or "I told you."
8. Walking away during a fight.
9. Leaving the toilet seat up or hair in the sink.
10. Not looking at me when I am talking (i.e. not listening).
11. Not changing the toilet tissue roll or using all of the toothpaste.

12. Expecting you to pay or to do the household chores.
13. Arguing in public.
14. Letting you make all of the decisions.
15. Being rude to other people (i.e. waitress or your family)

Are you waging war in relationships because of petty, passive, or pet peeves?

HIS HAIKUS

Haiku is a type of short-form poetry that originated in Japan. Traditional Japanese haiku consists of three phrases composed of 17 phonetic units in a 5, 7, 5 pattern.

Voluntary Unemployment
My now bride once said:
"You straighten up…not clean up!"
I now do neither.

Blind Date
Relationship Tip:
Trash cans just wanna be dumped.
It's not them. It's you.

Nights Like This…
Lights on. TV loud.
She needs this to fall asleep?!
Opposites attack!

They Wanna Be Down
P.S.A. Ladies:
Shower Heads or Toilet Seats?
One has to suffer.

Hot Take!
God sends us warnings.
Wife runs a heater year-round?
Please know: Hell is Real!

HER HAIKUS

Haiku is a type of short-form poetry that originated in Japan. Traditional Japanese haiku consist of three phrases composed of 17 phonetic units in a 5, 7, 5 pattern.

HOT-COLD BOLD
God Hear My Prayer
Hot is not Hot when I'm cold
I am freezing Dear!!!!

SNORING OUT MY HEART
Snoring symphonies
Plague my ears in surround sound
Quit! Sleeping! Beast-like!!!

THIS IS A STICK UP!
Hold the tube upright!
Bottom-up toothpaste pressure
Top-down methods suck!

BOOTY BOMB
Flipped toilet lids
Wet bottoms shock pink hearts
We don't pee standing!

ICE ICE CRAZY
Insanity is
Sixty-Five degrees ice-cold
Facts… It starts with you!

⌘

CHAPTER NINE
Ode To My Individual Relationship: Self-Love For Me, Myself, & I

TO THE MEN OF THIS ERA
AND THE AGE TO COME

First and foremost, thank you for taking the time to read this message (and hopefully this book). I understand that we must be cognizant and careful of the people we allow to speak into our lives. We live in a time where everyone touts themselves as an expert or guru worth adherence and emulation. I can reassure you that "this isn't that." The goal of this message is simply to offer you an opportunity for intentional self-reflection. I've learned that a good, effective method to assist in this important task is to utilize questions:

Question #1 - What is your motivation? Is it extrinsic or intrinsic? Do you have a vision of driving a certain car or living in a particular neighborhood? Maybe it's maintaining a specific lifestyle you want to provide for your family. It might be to disprove certain individuals who attempted to predict your future. Regardless of the answer, motivation represents the target that you're aiming to hit.

Question #2 - What is your mentality? If motivation is the destination, then mentality is the vehicle. It's how we get to where we are going. It speaks to our methodology and process. This is rooted in not only what we believe...but what we believe about ourselves.

Question #3 - How is your mettle? Many of us have the passion and intellect but lack the necessary discipline and stamina to fulfill our dreams. The depth of our mettle is proven when we encounter challenges and obstacles on the road to our desired future.

To be clear, I am not sharing all of this to convince you that I have mastered balancing the answers to these questions. I just want you to know that you are not alone in your struggles. One of the most important, yet underutilized tools that we as men have is partnership. That is my offer to you. Let's work together to ensure that we are walking in the proper motivation, mentality, and mettle to realize our destiny.

Submitted in Solidarity,
Walter "Wally B." Jennings

DEAR PHENOMENAL WOMEN OF TODAY AND BEYOND

Our great-grandmothers, grandmothers, and mothers were resilient, triumphant, and overcame trials and tribulations. Each has a rich legacy and a larger-than-life power story. Their idioms and advice echo loudly and proudly from generation to generation. The most profound is the sound of their silence. I am learning to be intrigued by silence and to pay more attention to what a woman is not saying or sharing. That definitely screams louder than any of her words. It is typically the birthplace of a wound, scab, scar, experience, or trauma. The silence can indicate that her inner child or young adult stopped speaking, growing, or reaching out because no one helped or heard. If the advice of the women elders before us missed your address, I want to encourage you with the following life-altering messages:

You are worthy! What is your worth? Reject all intrusive thoughts that you are not qualified enough. Ask yourself how I add value? No matter your education, socioeconomic status, who you know, and/or your traumatic past experiences, you are expensive. You are worth the price of Christ's blood. How much did that cost? It is impossible to quantify the value of this free sacrificial gift. No one is rich enough to repay that bounty and no one is bold enough to try, survive, and succeed.

You need the willpower to empower! Why does willpower matter? The most important two days of your life are the day you were born and the day you find out why (by Mark Twain). When you identify your purpose, it empowers you to persevere. This behavior encourages the younger generation and serves as an opportunity to mentor others. Trials will try to get in your way. If we lack the strength to say "no" to our current wants, needs, and desires, progress will slow down, and distractions may interrupt you from accomplishing long-term goals.

You are wiser than you think, specifically when you stop and think! How can wisdom manifest in challenging circumstances? Trust and obey the Lord and lean not to your own understanding (Psalms 3:5-6). The hardest thing for some personality types to do is trust and get quiet enough to listen and hear. Silence the soundtrack of your life and come to the end of yourself. Allow God to work and guide.

These three domains support the wellness of women overall. As an educator, life coach, mother, friend, and relationship coach, I have been called to challenge and change the worth, willpower, and wisdom of women. I work hard to practice what I teach and live what I believe. Let's get to work, ladies!

Sincerely Your Sister & Coach,
Charmaine 'C-Maine' Jennings

⌘
CHAPTER TEN
If I Knew Then...What I Know Now:
Words Of Wisdom

"Everyone is not going to be like you. Respect Individualism!"

"Allow your wife to evolve. Allow her to go off and learn."

"Communication is key. Whatever you do, do it in love."

Edward & Frances Jennings
60+Years Married

"Commit and take care of your family.
Trust and stand firm in the relationship that God joined together."

"Outside noises disable the inner circle from combining God-given resources. Inside voices demonstrate a peaceful transition."

"Before the marriage, it is important to put God first in order to begin the process of building your foundation.
Make sure God is in all decision-making."

Benjamin & Julia Smith
50+Years Married

"Challenges and struggles are excellent opportunities to build strength and resilience."

"Purpose is always anchored in belief."

"It is important to balance your self-work with collective responsibility."

Walter & Charmaine Jennings
20+Years Married

⌘

ABOUT THE AUTHORS

WALTER "WALLY B." JENNINGS

Walter "Wally B." Jennings is a native of Tampa, FL. He is a proven innovative instructional coach for business leaders and community stakeholders with 20+ years of experience in creative arts, operational management, and public event coordination. He specializes in pre-marital counseling, officiating wedding ceremonies, marriage intervention, individual life coaching, and youth development.

He is a graduate of Florida A&M University with a Bachelor's Degree in Business Economics.

Walter's arts-infused approach has earned him several national honors and awards as a program director, spoken-word artist, and venue host.

Walter is a husband of 20+ years, a proud father of 2 daughters, a son, brother, friend, and community leader devoted to exploring life lessons and compelling questions.

For more information, please visit WalterWallyBJennings.com or ChosenLifeSpecialists.com

CHARMAINE "C-MAINE" JENNINGS

Charmaine 'C-Maine' Jennings, is a West Palm Beach native. She is a stellar relationship coach and co-owner of Chosen Life Specialists, LLC. She is a poet, life coach, and artisan of creativity. She is a wife of 20+ years, mother of 2 daughters, advocate, and friend.

She is a veteran educator and began writing poetry as a teenager to deal with depression. She is a national trainer who excels at providing leadership coaching and professional learning opportunities for K-12 principals, coaches, teachers, and interventionists in Florida, Georgia, Indiana, Michigan, Missouri, Ohio, Alabama, Washington D.C., Texas, etc.

Charmaine is a change agent who utilizes arts-integrated strategies, poetry, and artful coaching. Her performances and creative works are typically a call to action that encourages personal growth and how to embrace uniqueness in order to overcome trauma and turn obstacles into opportunities. Learn more at CharmaineCmaineJennings.com or ChosenLifeSpecialists.com.

Purchase Your Copy

This 365-day artful guide to daily living seeks to captivate the soul, body, and mind in ways that verbal expression alone may limit. This experience will provoke you to think, create, and act. This art-infused approach supports emotional, spiritual, and social well-being, healing, and recovery through a person-centered approach. Get ready to dance, write, move, draw, cook, create, think, and most importantly...color the pages! Charmaine and Walter Jennings offer you 12 key principles on how to live a CHOSEN LIFE every day. This self-reflection and introspection tool supports personal growth and development, thus strengthening various areas of wellness and well-being.

Thank You!

We would like to extend a sincere thank you to our family, friends, church organizations, business partners, editor and publisher, volunteers, and emotional support partners for supporting us. We also thank you for purchasing this unique project. Please let us know how the stories, poetry, and components have impacted you personally. We appreciate your support and feedback is a gift.

May your relationships be successful and exceed your expectations. May you recover if/when the journey gets turbulent.

We are your Chosen Life Specialists!

"Called to Challenge and Change Relationship Culture"

For more details, please visit ChosenLifeSpecialists.com

CHOSEN LIFE SPECIALISTS, LLC